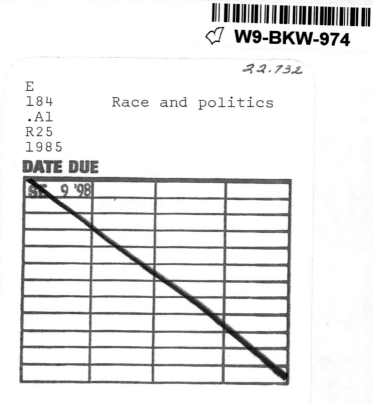

RACE AND POLITICS

edited by ELIZABETH BURGOYNE

THE REFERENCE SHELF

Volume 56 Number 6

THE H. W. WILSON COMPANY

New York   1985

THE REFERENCE SHELF

The books in this series contain reprints of articles, excerpts from books, and addresses on current issues and social trends in the United States and other countries. There are six separately bound numbers in each volume, all of which are generally published in the same calendar year. One number is a collection of recent speeches; each of the others is devoted to a single subject and gives background information and discussion from various points of view, concluding with a comprehensive bibliography. Books in the series may be purchased individually or on subscription.

Library of Congress Cataloging in Publication Data

Main entry under title:

Race and politics.

(The Reference shelf ; v. 56, no. 6)
Bibliography: p.
1. Minorities—United States—Political activity—Addresses, essays, lectures. 2. United States—Ethnic relations—Addresses, essays, lectures. 3. United States—Race relations—Addresses, essays, lectures.
I. Burgoyne, Elizabeth.
E184.A1R25   1985   305.8'00973   84-29174
ISBN 0-8242-0700-9

Printed in the United States of America

CONTENTS

PREFACE

The United States, as John F. Kennedy reminded us, is "a nation of immigrants," a society that constantly renews itself as it admits newcomers of every possible race, color, and national origin, and constantly ponders the question of how to build a unified country from the diverse elements of its population. The political struggle between classes and interests that can be observed in any democratic country is intensified in the United States by the factionalism of ethnic and racial groups.

During the 1920s and '30s the concept of a "melting pot" in which all ethnic groups would become Americanized, abandoning their distinctness and accepting others who had abandoned theirs, seemed to offer the best chance of achieving universal social equality. For many, perhaps all, of the European immigrant groups that arrived in the United States during the late nineteenth and early twentieth century, this concept became a reality as assimilation was followed by prosperity and political representation. By the 1960s, however, when Nathan Glazer and Daniel P. Moynihan published their classic study, *Beyond the Melting Pot* (1963), the pursuit of national homogeneity seemed neither possible nor desirable. For many ethnic groups, the melting process had not occurred, or had done so too slowly.

The past twenty years have seen the growth of ethnic voting blocs in which differences among various groups—in occupation, educational opportunity, and voting registration—have become the bases of political power. During this period the nation's largest racial minority groups, blacks and Hispanics, have made considerable political gains in mayoral and gubernatorial elections, so increasing the racial and cultural self-awareness of many voters, and bringing blacks and Hispanics to the polls in unprecedentedly large numbers.

The efforts of President Reagan's administration to reduce federal funding to programs that attempt to redress social inequities have also encouraged blacks and Hispanics to seek greater political representation.

It is the purpose of this compilation to survey a variety of opinions concerning racial equality, and present the political views of spokesmen for various racial groups. Since it would clearly be impossible to represent the full range of opinions in a volume of this size, the reader is advised to consult the bibliography for other points of view.

The compiler wishes to thank those authors and publishers who have given permission to reprint the selections in this book.

ELIZABETH BURGOYNE

February 1985

I. AFFIRMATIVE DISCRIMINATION: ETHNIC POLITICS

EDITOR'S INTRODUCTION

E Pluribus Unum, the motto inscribed on the Great Seal of the United States, would be just as appropriate if its meaning were reversed, *Ex Uno Pluris,* many from one. The merging of the many sub-nationalities of American society, differentiated by race, religion, or language, in the melting pot of a national character seems to be indefinitely postponed until the day when every group believes it has received its economic due. Desire for pluralism rather than homogeneity was officially recognized by the 1980 Census form, which asks respondents to identify their ancestry by one of fifteen categories.

As William Peterson points out in the first article in this section, reprinted from the *National Review,* the current trend in American ethnic politics is to ask "What's in it for us?" John Herbers, reporting on the Democratic primary campaign in the *New York Times,* takes a sardonic look at the efforts of candidates to trim their views to suit the interests of various ethnic groups, and an article from *Newsweek* claims that the notion of the melting pot is very much out of fashion. Finally, a *Washington Post* article by Michael Barone says that in their efforts to attract the ethnic vote, both major parties, despite their differences, find it effective to evoke the emotional connotations of Ellis Island, symbol of immigrant struggles and aspirations.

ETHNIC POLITICS[1]

In Europe the definition of *nation* is closely tied to the word's etymology: a nation comprises the present descendants of a putative ancestor. No such physical bond, however, could have been postulated to unite the diverse peoples of the American colonies, and the nation that evolved out of them was based on political principle rather than accident of birth. Those who formally accepted the doctrines of democratic liberty and justice could become American citizens and, whatever their prior status, pass on this identity to their children. (Even today, European intellectuals often find it difficult to understand this distinction. In particular, many consider it laughable if not outrageous to denote certain activities as "un-American." For what could the meaning be of, say, accusing a Swede of "un-Swedish activities"? Every Swede is defined by his blood, and whatever he does is Swedish.) It was the magnet of political and social democracy rather than any government policy that enabled the new U.S.A. to realize its motto of *E pluribus unum*—"Out of many, one." The "melting pot" has been a target of liberal attack for so many years that the actual policy associated with that slogan has been all but forgotten.

First, one should recall that full acculturation was not only the government's intention but also the typical aspiration of the immigrants themselves. Not incidentally, the phrase derived from a highly successful bit of kitsch by the Anglo-Jewish writer Israel Zangwill. The story of *The Melting Pot* revolves around the marriage between the Jewish hero and the daughter of the Czarist official responsible for the pogrom in which the hero's father was murdered. For in the New World—this was the play's message—all the ancient hatreds would disappear through a literal mixing of the races. And by any criterion except utopian precision, the American melting pot *has* worked. Compared to those in any other major receiving country, ethnic strains in the United States have

[1]Reprint of an article by William Peterson, Robert Lazarus Professor of Social Demography at Ohio State University. *National Review.* 30:92–4. Ja. 20, '78. Copyright © 1978 by National Review, Inc., 150 East 35 Street, New York, N.Y. 10016. Reprinted with permission.

generally moved toward a common center, not necessarily losing their identity but softening it sufficiently to become genuinely parts of a single whole.

In the early 1930s, when I was an undergraduate, even to utter such a phrase as "the Jewish vote" or "the Polish vote" marked one as a reactionary. According to the prevalent myth, ethnic politics did not exist. I found this excessive delicacy somewhat absurd, not because I was less naïve than the typical student, but because my upbringing had taught me that in some circumstances voting by ethnic blocs could determine the outcome of political conflict.

Splitting the Loot

Jersey City, where I was born and raised, could be described with equal truth as the home of one of the last of the old-style political machines that long dominated American municipal politics, or as an early version of the welfare state. Elections were rigged; as a Republican poll-watcher, I once discovered that every adult resident of a 12-family apartment house that had burned to the ground a decade earlier had continued to vote Democratic from that address as well as from at least one other.

Over the years, however, it became less and less necessary to steal elections so crudely. Each of the city's social services was established partly for the benefits it brought the people, but mainly for the concomitant benefits it brought the Democratic Party. The construction and maintenance of a public hospital, extraordinarily large and sumptuously equipped, imposed mammoth political debts on contractors and subcontractors, on physicians, nurses, and ancillary staff, and particularly on the many who received medical care without having to pay for it. Eventually, the portion of the city's electorate "on the titty," as the phrase went, together with their families, friends, and personal beneficiaries, probably constituted a legitimate majority. Stuffing the ballot boxes continued only as insurance against mishap—as well as out of sheer momentum to give the boys something to do on election day.

In my childhood, Jersey City was about four-fifths Roman Catholic and the Catholic nationalities ran the city. As in New York and Boston and other Eastern cities, the Irish held almost all the top positions in government and its various offshoots. Italians, who had immigrated later, had acquired control of, for instance, the lucrative franchise to collect and dispose of garbage: from department director to wagon driver, this was their monopoly. Poles were also on the team, but as more junior partners. Then there were people like my father, a lower-middle-class Protestant; and Jews; and—several steps down—Negroes. By and large, our role was to pay our taxes and not expect too much for them.

Why was it that in their relations with the Federal Government voters were supposed to act as ethnically undifferentiated Americans, while the units of city politics were obviously and unashamedly ethnic blocs? One reason, certainly, was that as guardian of our relations with other countries the United States Government was more sensitive to the double identities of immigrants and their descendants. But the principal reason, I believe, was that the functions of local governments could entail the distribution of favors to those with sufficient influence. An individual can cast a vote, but he is seldom able to exert the pressure needed to obtain preferential treatment from a party machine. For that he must organize into units—but into smaller units than the heterogeneous American-style party—and one obvious base for mustering power was social clubs organized with a quasi-political purpose. The development of ethnicity into a combative stance, in short, derived from the power of the state to allocate goods and services, leading to what is known in the current euphemism as the welfare state.

Dual Loyalty

This standard pattern in East Coast cities became a prototype for federal practice. As an important member of the Democratic Party's national committee, Jersey City's Mayor Frank Hague influenced the development of the New Deal. Partly under the tutelage of such big-city associates, Franklin Roosevelt succeeded in adapting the Tammany model to the larger stage of national politics; in particular, he succeeded in shifting the Negro vote, very heavily Republican in honor of that party's anti-slavery origins, to virtually totally Democratic. By the 1940s it was becoming respectable to refer openly to the political role of American nationalities.

During earlier decades, the literary metaphor of the melting pot had been elaborated by liberal academics. With his associates and students at the University of Chicago, Professor Robert Park developed the thesis that all interethnic relations go through an invariable and irreversible four-stage succession: contact, competition, accommodation, and assimilation. This conventional theory was applied specifically to black-white relations in Gunnar Myrdal's *An American Dilemma,* which is a convenient summary of the doctrine.

Differences between the races, according to Myrdal, were of three types: real but superficial differences (e.g., skin color), false stereotypes (e.g., the "lower intelligence" of blacks), and the results of discriminatory institutions (e.g., the lower level of basic skills acquired in poorer schools). By what Myrdal termed a "principle of cumulation," any improvement in Negroes' real situation would raise whites' perception of them, and vice versa. As blacks rose economically, the cultural differences between the races as perceived from either side would diminish and eventually become altogether insignificant. Nothing in this whole assimilationist doctrine prepared Americans for what actually happened: the response to the great improvement in Negroes' economic and civil condition was a massive resurgence of Afro-American separatism.

Meanwhile the melting-pot thesis had been subjected to partial but gradually increasing emendation. Early on, Horace Kallen argued for "cultural pluralism," the retention of those old-country traits consistent with political loyalty. This compromise was mainly a defense against the nativist pressure for national quotas in the immigration laws of the 1920s. The demand for autonomy was carried one step further in Samuel Lubell's influential book, *The Future of American Politics* (1952), which interpreted the positions of "interventionists" and "isolationists" as deriving from vestigial loyalties to, respectively, England and Germany. The charge of dual loyalty, which immigrants answered in earlier decades with a flat denial, was now excused with a blanket *tu quoque.* The new view reached a kind of climax in

Will Herberg's division of American sub-nations into
Protestant–Catholic–Jew, whose numbers in 1955, when the book
was published, were approximately 79 million, 31 million, and
under four million. Within one generation, if we accept these
books as representative, American Jews went from a joyful antici-
pation of their disappearance into native American society to a demand for full corporate equality with the far larger sub-nations
of the earlier settlers. Being both highly vulnerable and of above-
average intelligence, Jews had been the first to develop a rationale
for group autonomy. Not surprisingly, spokesmen for other minorities began to follow the same route to something like the same
conclusions.

Exaggerations

It has now become utterly routine to analyze all election returns by ethnicity, but this complete reversal of former practice
certainly often exaggerates the ethnic factor in individuals' votes.
The facts on which the new dogma is based are dubious. Since the
vote is secret, we lack full data relating any characteristic to what
psephomancers term voting behavior. Statistics are by precincts,
and area correlations are truly convincing only in the exceptional
case in which one compares, say, wards populated only by Jews
with wards populated only by Irish Catholics (but then are people
who live in such enclaves typical of the Jews or Irish Catholics
who live among outsiders?). Thus, most of our supposed information comes from opinion polls, whose samples are typically too
small to permit us, with very much confidence in the results, to
break them down into sub-categories. In a word, the current ideology that Americans vote in large part as a reflection of their race
or nationality or religion is partly true, but may be no more true
than the onetime dictum that ethnicity exercises no influence at
all on voting.

Both of these ideologies have now been given official sanction,
and our problems can be summed up by citing the fact that the
law requires, simultaneously, two contradictory responses from
local governments, business firms, and universities. The discovery
of two diverse modes of ending, or at least mitigating, discrimina-

tion against blacks led not to a choice of one or the other, but to the enforcement of both.

Lewis to Carmichael

The determination to establish color-blind justice in the United States, though long frustrated, had achieved some notable successes in the years following the Second World War. As a consequence of this program, civil rights activists fought with heightened intensity. Within two or three years, the demands voiced in Birmingham and the COFO (Council of Federated Organizations) voting campaign in Mississippi (1963–64) had culminated in race riots in six cities (1964) and the super-riot of Watts (1965). Undoubtedly the Civil Rights Act of 1964, the most substantial and comprehensive bill outlawing discrimination since Reconstruction, was passed partly to quell the rioting, which nevertheless continued to expand. Justice granted tardily as an answer to blackmail was tarnished, and the campaign to establish it was transformed into something quite different. In 1966, John Lewis gave way to Stokely Carmichael as head of SNCC; this change symbolized a total reversal in both tactics and purpose. In its new form, the bi-racial SNCC became a centralized body openly espousing violence to achieve black-nationalist ends.

The pattern of granting blacks rather than whites preferential treatment in hiring or promotion, access to colleges or professional schools, and other scarce values is clearly contrary to both the civil rights tradition and the law in which that tradition is most fully embodied. Not only does the Civil Rights Act of 1964 prohibit discrimination in general, but, for instance, it also provides, with respect to the business world, that "nothing contained in this title should be interpreted to require any employer . . . to grant preferential treatment to any individual or to any group because of race, color, religion, sex, or national origin . . . on account of an imbalance which may exist with respect to the total number or percentage."

If the language were not sufficiently clear, it was spelled out on the floor of Congress by Senators Joseph Clark and Clifford Case, who acted as the bill's floor managers: "The question in

each case is whether that *individual* was discriminated against."
"Quotas are themselves discriminatory." Nevertheless, corporations have since been required to meet numerical goals in the hiring and promotion of certain "minorities" (including women, who
constitute a majority, but excluding some ethnic minorities who
have suffered serious group deprivations, such as Appalachian
whites). Firms have been heavily penalized on the basis of statisti-
cal evidence alone. For example, the so-called Equal Employment
Opportunity Commission forced AT&T to give some tens of millions of dollars in back pay to minority employees even though no
act of discrimination by the company against any individual em-
ployee was ever admitted or proved.

If "affirmative discrimination," as Nathan Glazer calls it, is
clearly against statutory law, how has it become the dominant
horn of our dilemma? It is because the courts, and federal bureaus
with the courts' approval, have taken to writing laws that super-
sede those of Congress. By failing to clarify basic principles under-
lying the law of ethnic relations, the courts have permitted a dual
system of law to proliferate.

A prime instance of both injustice and judicial cowardice is the
notorious De Funis case. A white Jewish member of Phi Beta
Kappa with a high B average in undergraduate courses, Marco
De Funis applied for admission to the University of Washington's
law school and was turned down. A year later, his score of 668
in the Law School Aptitude Test put him in the top 7 per cent of
those seeking to enter the school. When again he was not admitted,
De Funis sued the university, charging that its policy of giving
preference to less qualified minority applicants had deprived him
of equal protection. He won in the lower court and was admitted
to law school, but the state Supreme Court supported the university's appeal. In a second appeal, the U.S. Supreme Court heard ar-
guments but then refused to hand down a decision on the ground
that, since the plaintiff was by that time in the last year of law
school, the case was moot. The somewhat similar case of Allan
Bakke is now before the Court.

The victims of this policy include not only some whites, but
many Negroes as well. Consider the man of color—whether black,
Chicano, American Indian, or whatever—who on the basis of gen-

uine achievement managed against heavy odds to raise himself and his family to middle-class respectability, and who now sees the belief spread that he got where he is solely on the basis of his color.

Ethnic Splinters

Until very recently, Americans have thought of discrimination as anything which inhibited the efforts of minorities to acculturate fully; elsewhere, discrimination usually referred to attempts by the state to eliminate the language, religion, or other distinctive elements of a self-conscious sub-nation. The hope of the civil rights movement of a generation ago was that discrimination of the first type could be eliminated; instead, the victimization has merely been shifted to other sectors of the population. The resultant marshaling of ethnic blocs, whether to achieve new victories or to defend the traditional norms of justice, suggests a new pattern for American society.

The Black Caucus in Congress is now being imitated by Chicano congressmen, who announce that they too will discuss all bills from the point of view of "what's in it for us?" As these instances suggest, in a country with so diverse a population the welfare state can be much more destructive of the social fabric than in homogeneous Sweden. If the fissiparous trends ever develop to the intensity already evident in Britain, Belgium, or several other Western democracies, little in the country will remain recognizable. Yet what shall we expect from the graduates of Black Studies Programs and their various offshoots (there are six such programs at UCLA) but a continuing effort to split the country into its ethnic splinters? After all, we have trained them for nothing else.

ETHNIC DIVISIONS SURFACE IN THE CAMPAIGN[2]

It has been a long time since ethnic, racial and religious divisions have been so pronounced in a Presidential campaign. As the contest to select a Democratic opponent to President Reagan passes its halfway mark, the forces bringing the conflicts to the surface seem far from spent.

Polarization, of course, has been most visible in the highly publicized rift between the Rev. Jesse Jackson and Jews. His reference, before the New Hampshire primary, to Jews as "hymies" is considered a major blunder that damaged his ambitious effort to build a "rainbow coalition" of various races and groups. Not only Jews but other whites have shunned his rainbow; he has taken less than 7 percent of the white vote so far.

But in increasing numbers blacks have flocked to his banner —50 percent of those registered in Alabama, 61 percent in Georgia and 79 percent in Illinois. They have done so despite their acknowledgement in many cases that Mr. Jackson cannot win the nomination and that his candidacy is hurting Walter F. Mondale, the white candidate whom most blacks prefer to oppose Mr. Reagan. The Amsterdam News, a black weekly in New York City, decided not to endorse either and simply urged its readers to make their own choice between the two, but to vote by all means to "show the thunder of our numbers."

Another sign of the increasing sensitivity was that both the former Vice President and Senator Gary Hart opened their campaigns for Tuesday's New York primary with a promise to move the United States Embassy in Israel from Tel Aviv to Jerusalem —a peripheral but potentially explosive issue that Administrations of both parties have felt better left in the background, because it might arouse Arab violence and further deter Middle East peace. (Calling the proposal "unwise," President Reagan last week said he would veto a long-pending bill that would accomplish the move.)

[2]Reprint of an article by John Herbers. *New York Times.* p E 5. Ap. 1, '84. Copyright © 1984 by The New York Times Company. Reprinted by permission.

Howard I. Friedman, president of the American Jewish Committee, spoke for many Jewish leaders when he called the focus on the Embassy move a "caricature presentation" not "rooted in an entire range of (Jews') traditional concerns." Jews "don't want to be patronized by just being talked to about Israel," he added. But the two candidates were clearly appealing to the intensified support among American Jews for Israel, just as Senator Hart was appealing to heightened Irish sensitivities when he promised to appoint a special panel to promote the unity of Ireland.

John A. Kromkowski, president of the National Center for Ethnic Affairs, and other experts, agree that more than the usual ethnic politics is involved in this year's Presidential race. The groups themselves are more restless, more concerned about the future and their place in American politics, said Mr. Kromkowski, who concentrates on mediating differences among white communities that have strong ethnic identifications.

Much of the new anxiety has not yet been reflected in Presidential politics. But there is other evidence of it—for example, the manner in which the Portuguese communities reacted last month in New Bedford and Fall River, Mass., to the rape trial of six men, all Portuguese. Many interpreted the trial and the verdict as a vendetta rather than criminal justice. And while there have been signs of healing between blacks and whites in some places, such as Philadelphia and Boston, there are many other communities like Chicago, where deep racial antagonism is dramatized daily within the city government.

Rick Reidy, who works with ethnic groups for the Democratic National Committee, said that in his travels around the country he had found an increase in conflicts "with group pitted against group." "There is a lot less caring," he said, attributing the change, as could be expected, to what he characterized as President Reagan's divisive leadership. His counterparts on the Republican National Committee take the opposite view, that Mr. Reagan has been a healing force.

Yet many people agree that the Reagan factor is implicated in the feelings of insecurity. As Mr. Kromkowski notes, many members of ethnic groups left their political moorings in 1980. Virtually all of them had traditionally been Democrats, seeking to redress their grievances through that party. Four years ago, many of them voted for Mr. Reagan. European ethnic blue-collar groups, in particular, seem uncertain which way to go in a nation whose economy and institutions are rapidly changing.

Immigration Friction

The new politicization of blacks, who were relatively inert in 1980, stems largely from their perception that President Reagan has damaged them through his curtailment of social and civil right programs, a perception that has made Mr. Jackson's candidacy possible. Israel's invasion of Lebanon and other developments in the Middle East, where the Reagan Administration has been unable to score a policy victory, have increased the intensity of feeling among American Jews about Israel. And the conflicts between Mr. Jackson and other black leaders and the Jewish community stem at least in part from some blacks' favoring the Palestinians in the increasingly corrosive Middle Eastern conflict.

Adding to the friction is the fact that the United States is once again undergoing waves of immigration by people of different color and traditions than the majority. Recent population growth has been based on an influx of Latins and Asians. There is now no cry of a "yellow peril" about Chinese or the rise of a "Know Nothing" party to restrict immigration, as there was in the 1850's. But there is heightened competition for economic and social advantage. Like protective tariffs and prayer in the public schools, issues once considered settled are alive again, and differences between ethnic, racial and religious groups keep forcing their way into the political contests, even if in different forms.

THE POLITICS OF ETHNICITY[3]

The most interesting result of Jimmy Carter's remarks on "ethnic purity" was not so much the fuss over his wording as the fact that most of the Presidential aspirants turned out to agree with his policy. None of the candidates favors Federal initiatives to break up ethnic neighborhoods (though most would step in to stop housing discrimination). In the post-liberal politics of 1976, ethnicity is very much in and the melting pot is very much out. The last decade has brought a new sense of ethnic pride and awareness in the U.S., and politicians have done considerable homage to the country's ethnic subcultures.

When a social trend like this is discerned, academic researchers are quick to fasten onto it, and in some cases they have been the first to do the discerning. Spurred on by grants from the Rockefeller and Ford foundations, scholars have embarked on dozens of ethnic-research projects. In 1972, Congress gave its own blessing to ethnic scholarship by passing the Ethnic Heritage Studies Act, which authorized $15 million for research. The research has turned up some interesting—and often surprising—judgments about the political views and impact of American ethnic groups.

Myths

According to political sociologist Richard Hamilton of Canada's McGill University, ethnic ties are the main influence on voting behavior. In his book "Restraining Myths," published last year, Hamilton argues that a person's contacts with his family, school, church and neighborhood are more important in determining his political outlook than his economic status or any other factor.

As expected, ethnic cohesiveness is strongest in traditional neighborhoods. Yet, Hamilton finds, ethnic ties persist even in the

[3]Reprint of an article by Kenneth L. Woodward. Newsweek 87:53. Ap. 26, '76. Copyright © 1976, by Newsweek, Inc. All rights reserved. Reprinted by permission.

newer suburbs where third-generation families still tend to social-
ize with people of the same ethnic and religious background.
Thus, despite upward mobility, Hamilton reports that white
Protestants tend to be the most conservative group at every income
level, and Catholics tend to be more liberal than any other group
except Jews.

Hamilton also finds that upper-middle-class elites, who seem
culturally assimilated, actually follow many of the same instincts
as neighborhood ethnics. These elites, he argues, grow up in similar suburbs, attend the same privileged schools and live in similarly affluent enclaves. In fact, writes Hamilton, it was the elite
readers of the elite publications—mainly the white Protestants—
who were the most hawkish in their support of the Vietnam war.
They were also the group most affected by the mass media's eventual turn against that war in the late '60s. "They, in short, 'came
around' to the moderate blue-collar position," Hamilton concludes.

The block-voting habits of the working classes were analyzed
by Mark Levy and Michael Kramer in "The Ethnic Factor," published in 1972. Reviewing a dozen years of election returns from
2,000 precincts, the authors found that white ethnics were so tied
by tradition to the Democratic Party that they generally voted for
Democrats even when the candidate took some positions more liberal than their own. Slavic-Americans, for example, are the least
assimilated white ethnic group and the closest to blacks at the lower economic levels, yet they consistently produced healthy majorities for liberal Democrats. Even Irish-Americans, the most
assimilated of the white ethnics, supported Democratic candidates
by a margin of 2 to 1.

Sociologist Andrew Greeley, director of the Center for the
Study of American Pluralism in Chicago, has also offered impressive evidence that the hyphenated American is not a reactionary
hard-hat. In "Ethnicity in the United States," published in 1974,
Father Greeley presented statistics to measure the response of
white ethnics—mainly Irish, Italian and Slavic Catholics—
against those of "mainstream America" on key social issues. Greeley reported that the Catholic ethnics were more likely than other
Americans (except Jews) to have opposed the war in Vietnam

from the outset; that after the Watergate revelations, they turned against former President Richard Nixon earlier and more strongly than did other segments of the population, and that they were less likely than the average Democratic voter to defect from the party when liberal Sen. George McGovern was its Presidential nominee in 1972. Unfortunately, Greeley concluded, the political liberalism of white ethnics had escaped notice by intellectuals and journalists because the latter had willfully misinterpreted the ethnic factor in U.S. politics.

Sociologists Nathan Glazer and Daniel Patrick Moynihan—a political figure himself—published a controversial essay in Commentary magazine in October 1974 that offered several reasons why the politics of white ethnics have been misunderstood by liberal intellectuals. White ethnic solidarity, they argued, confounds the "liberal expectancy" that the emphasis on individual achievement in modern societies dilutes the ties of family and ethnic heritage.

Class

Ethnic cohesiveness also flies in the face of another theory favored by liberal intellectuals—the Marxist assumption that class interests based on economic status overshadow differences based upon religion, language and other ethnic attachments. As it turns out, said Moynihan and Glazer, the modern American welfare state has forced ethnics to function as economic self-interest groups in order to achieve a larger slice of government benefits.

It also seems likely that liberals have misunderstood white ethnics because they have seen them in juxtaposition to blacks—the whites' neighborhood cohesion, their clustering in schools and jobs have all been too glibly regarded as symptoms of racial bias. One of the main contributions of the new research on ethnicity has been to focus on the positive, rather than negative, side of white ethnic solidarity. And that is one of the reasons that politicians besides George Wallace now find it acceptable to cultivate the ethnic voter again.

THE BATTLE FOR ELLIS ISLAND[4]

To understand the first weeks of campaigning after the Democratic convention, consider this fact: more than half of all Americans are descended from immigrants who came over in the great waves of migration from 1840 to 1920. What we are seeing, from Ronald Reagan and from Walter Mondale and Geraldine Ferraro, all of them products of that migration, is the battle for Ellis Island.

It's a mistake to see this as just a contest for one ethnic group or another. It's true that the selection of Ferraro will get some Italian-Americans to vote Democratic who would otherwise have voted without thinking much about it for Reagan; it's probably true also that Reagan's Irish ancestry works for him.

But those are marginal effects. Mario Cuomo, as the Democratic candidate for governor of New York in 1982, running against a Jewish conservative Republican, won only 51 percent of the Italian-American vote, the same percentage as his statewide percentage. When voting for candidates for state treasurer or judge, many voters will do as a woman I canvassed in Boston put it: "I just go down the ballot and vote for all the good Irish names." But that's not how they choose presidents and vice presidents.

What's important in 1984 is not how each ticket appeals to specific ethnic groups, but which is more successful in appealing to the Ellis Island tradition generally. For most Americans, Ellis Island is a living memory—not something they experienced themselves, but something they have heard about from parents or grandparents, part of the family lore and tradition. They know that the people before them came over with nothing, often not even knowing English. They know that they worked, more hours a day than most Americans today can imagine; they struggled, in living and working conditions most Americans today would not tolerate for a minute. They lived in smelly, tiny, airless apartments, endured the prejudice of others. And they succeeded, in spite of it

[4]Reprint of an article by Michael Barone, editorial staff writer. *Washington Post*. Ag. 14, '84. Copyright © 1984 The Washington Post.

all. Because of their efforts, their grandchildren and great-grandchildren are more prosperous and comfortable and secure than they ever could have imagined. "We stand," Mario Cuomo likes to say, "on the shoulders of giants."

Ronald Reagan, who grew up as an Irish-American in mostly Yankee Dixon, Ill., understands Ellis Island. It may have seemed hokey and imitative for him to campaign this year at St. Ann's in Hoboken, N.J., just after Mondale picked Ferraro and campaigned with her in Queens. But Reagan began his 1980 campaign not far away in Jersey City, in sight of the Statue of Liberty. And he articulated then, and often has since, a vision of America as a land of opportunity and tolerance for immigrants. He has a generous impulse toward today's immigrants as well, and toward Latin America, where so many of them come from. In the 1980 campaign he consistently refused to exploit the hot feelings existing then against Cuban refugees, and in his early speeches he advocated a common market for Latin America and the Caribbean.

Of course Reagan's generosity isn't the same as the Democrats'. He thinks government regulation and aid stifle economic growth, and in his version of Ellis Island the immigrants' success was possible because of, not despite, the free market and free enterprise. He wants to see such experiences replicated with today's immigrants and in today's Latin America, as he thinks they are in today's East Asia. There is a lot in history to support his views.

But there's also a lot to support the Democrats' version, in which a compassionate government, like a compassionate head of the family, stepped in and helped the people who went through Ellis Island achieve success. Government regulated working conditions, starting with the response to the Triangle Fire of 1911; it revived the economy, in the 1930s and 1940s, and provided unemployment insurance; it provided aid to the helpless; it protected individuals against cheating and poisoning by giant businesses. It helped people working their way up in the world go to college (the GI Bill) and buy their own homes (FHA mortgage guarantees). It took the potentially radical masses of Ellis Island and made them into conservative-minded, community-nurturing, middle-class homeowners.

There is probably less difference between the Reagan and
Mondale policies than the contrast between these two visions suggests. Reagan is not likely to dismantle the American makeshift
welfare state in a second term, and Mondale is not likely to make
it much larger. But the two versions of Ellis Island at least suggest
the direction of the changes each would try to make. Ellis Island
does not resonate for all Americans; the Ellis Island experience
is foreign to all blacks, almost all white southerners, and a good
many Protestants. Neither Jesse Jackson nor Gary Hart has any
feel for it, and unlike Hart's vision of a technocratic future it is
much more a vivid description of the past than a forecast of the
future.

But in the big northern states, where much of this election will
be fought, Ellis Island is a vibrant tradition for most voters now.
Only 24 years ago millions of voters were frightened by the possibility that the nation would elect a president who was a product
of the 1840–1920 migration. Today it is the Ellis Island tradition
that both parties resort to in trying to bind together enough of the
culturally diverse groups that make up America's majority today.

EDITOR'S INTRODUCTION

On August 28, 1963, the Reverend Martin Luther King Jr., speaking from the steps of the Lincoln Memorial in Washington, D.C., attacked racial discrimination in his famous speech, "I Have a Dream." "I have a dream that one day this nation will rise up and live out the true meaning of its creed: 'We hold these truths self-evident, that all men are created equal.'"

How much of King's dream had come true twenty years later? The Voting Rights Act of 1965 removed many of the discriminatory practices that hindered blacks from voting. In 1964 there were only 280 elected black officials in the entire country; in 1982 there were 5,160. By 1984 many major cities, including Los Angeles, Chicago, and Philadelphia, had black mayors. The importance of black political participation on behalf of white Democratic candidates was strikingly evident in the victory of Governor Mario Cuomo of New York, who gathered only 44 per cent of white votes, but 88 per cent of black votes.

During the 1984 Democratic primary campaign, however, there were signs that many blacks had become disenchanted with the Democratic Party, the choice of an overwhelming majority of black voters since the New Deal. This discontent was loudly voiced by Jesse Jackson, who was angered by the failure of white Democrats to vote for a black Democratic Party candidate in the Chicago mayoral election in 1983. Jackson's bid for the Democratic presidential nomination in 1984 gave blacks a new confidence in their political power and forced white politicians to pay greater attention to the needs of the black community.

Jackson's dramatic rise to prominence as a national political leader was owed in part, however, to causes that seem likely to sustain the alliance between black voters and the Democratic Party through the 1984 presidential election. For instance, the Reagan administration, which in the three years following its election had brought about many budget cuts in federal programs that assisted the poor, was widely regarded as hostile to the black cause, and this perception was strengthened by an economic recession that in 1983 drove unemployment among blacks to over twenty per cent.

In an article reprinted from the *New York Times Magazine,* Paul Delaney surveys black political activity on a national scale, showing that after a period of disillusion that followed the success of the Civil Rights movement, blacks "rediscovered the power of the ballot." Then Julian Bond, State Senator from Georgia, in a 1983 speech reprinted from *Negro History Bulletin,* argues that despite the risk of dividing the Democratic vote, the black community should have a presidential candidate. In the third article, reprinted from the *Nation,* Andrew Kopkind regards Jackson's candidacy as an unprecedented event in American politics, a movement that extends beyond the notion of "black power" toward an alliance of all those who regard themselves as unfairly treated by the economic system.

VOTING: THE NEW BLACK POWER[1]

Paine College, in Augusta, Ga., is one of those small, perennially troubled black schools that seem somehow to survive, if not thrive. Its weather-beaten, red-brick buildings contrast sharply with the modern structures across the street at predominantly white Georgia Medical College—striking symbolism given the history of inequities between blacks and whites in the South.

Recently, five young volunteers set up headquarters in Paine's student center, manning a long table positioned near the entrance. Their mission was voter registration—of at least 100 freshmen and returning students in four hours. They conducted sweeps of the campus, literally dragging students in. In one sweep, they

[1]Reprint of an article by Paul Delaney, deputy national news editor of the *New York Times. New York Times Magazine.* N. 27, '83. Copyright © 1983 by The New York Times Company. Reprinted by permission.

pulled in members of the school's starting basketball team. Once seated at the table, most of the registrants commented on how they had intended to sign up sooner.

Lisa Jones, the smallest but most aggressive of the five workers, spotted a prospective candidate.

"Are you registered?" she asked Charles E. Beamon, a shy 19-year-old freshman from Marietta.

"No, but I'd like to be," he answered.

Miss Jones led him to the table and began filling out the blue registration form.

"You haven't been convicted of a felony, have you?" she asked dutifully, but with a laugh that made the question less offensive.

"No," he drawled, returning the laugh.

Asked afterward why he was registering to vote now, a year after he had become eligible, Beamon said: "I don't like the way the country's being run, and my vote could make a difference. It won't make or break a man, but it will count. And I want to get rid of Reagan."

The scene at Paine College, where the campaign volunteers exceeded their goal of registering 100 people, is evidence that even before the Rev. Jesse L. Jackson officially entered the Presidential race this month, the political atmosphere in America's black community was highly charged. The episode is representative of what is happening in many parts of the country. If sustained, the current voter-registration drives, and, more important, the actual turnout for the primaries and general election next year, could make the black vote as important and as crucial as many politicians, leaders and analysts predict it will be.

Reversing trends that saw a decline in voting among both the black and white electorates, the turnout by blacks has surged since 1978. And in 1980, voting by blacks increased by nearly 2 percent from the 1976 figure, ending 20 years of steady decline in national elections. Between 1980 and 1982, the names of an additional 573,000 blacks have gone on the rolls, and since the summer of 1982 an additional 600,000 have been added, propelling black registration to 10,422,000, according to a report prepared by the Joint Center for Political Studies, a Washington research organization funded by various foundations and Government grants. In total, there are 17.6 million blacks of voting age, most concentrated in Northern and Southern cities.

More and more blacks have begun to participate in the electoral process as candidates, voters and volunteers. Some sections of many urban areas look and feel almost as they did during the civil-rights movement two decades ago. Indeed, some people even refer to the new political activity as a crusade; others use the term "the movement."

The principal reason for this renewed interest in politics is not the subject of much debate: the worsening conditions of many black Americans under the Reagan Administration and its conservative policies. The Census Bureau and other surveys have found that much of the momentum behind the progress made by blacks during the last two decades was effectively halted by last year. The black unemployment rate is still double that for whites; the median income of black families is about half that for whites, and the percentage of blacks living below the poverty line, which had been declining, has risen 15 percent since 1965, to the highest figure in 17 years. The Census Bureau suggested that among the contributing factors to the increase were the recession and, possibly, new Federal restrictions on eligibility for public assistance.

The Reagan Administration also has gone to court to oppose affirmative action and school and job integration orders that a few years ago would have found the Government and civil-rights lawyers on the same side. More than any other segment of American society, blacks feel, rightly or wrongly, that they have been singled out by an Administration with little understanding of or sympathy for their plight. Many of them believe they have borne the brunt of its drive to reduce the budget and the Federal role in governing the country. They also believe that President Reagan and his Administration are hostile to their interests. And the hostility is mutual. In contrast to the riots of the 1960's, however, blacks are not reacting by marching or with violence. They are rediscovering the power of the ballot. And Jesse Jackson's entry into Presidential politics has added an extra incentive as a symbol of discontent.

The Cleveland of the 1960's that Sarah Short Austin, executive director of the Greater Cleveland Roundtable and former executive vice president of the National Urban Coalition, remembers was a city trying to live up to its motto, "Best Location in the Nation." That was when she was a student at Case-Western Reserve University. Cleveland's shaded boulevards and quiet side streets attracted thousands of blacks, who left the South to work in the city's steel mills and automobile plants. The city, considered progressive by many, in 1966 was the first of its size to elect a black man as mayor: Carl Stokes.

Yet since then, many sections of Cleveland have come to resemble a battleground. The city's pock-marked streets, deteriorating downtown and neighborhoods, and acute racial tensions in the early 1970's earned it a notoriety that made it the butt of urban jokes rivaling W. C. Fields's about Philadelphia. So embattled was Stokes with both his black and white constituents, much of it his own fault, that he did not seek reelection.

The Greater Cleveland Roundtable, which Mrs. Austin heads, is a coalition of civic, religious, minority, labor and business leaders seeking solutions, with some success, to the city's myriad problems. Redevelopment is taking place in some downtown areas. Racial tension has been lessened.

Blacks in Cleveland and elsewhere have developed a sophisticated political strength. Today there are black mayors of Chicago, Los Angeles and Philadelphia, the nation's second-, third- and fourth-largest cities, respectively. Recently, blacks have won mayoral campaigns in Flint, Mich., and Charlotte, N.C. In Boston this month, Melvin H. King became the first black in the city's history to reach the final stage in the mayoral election. Approximately 240 blacks are mayors throughout the country; 350 blacks have been elected to state legislatures, and altogether, more than 5,400 blacks hold elected office. In Cleveland, 10 of the 21-member City Council are blacks, including the president, George L. Forbes.

"In the continuing struggle to enter fully into the mainstream," says Mrs. Austin, "it is in the arena of politics that blacks find the leadership and power that are denied them in the economic area."

Jesse Jackson is riding the crest of this wave of black political activity. The message of his candidacy and of the voter-registration drive generally is clear and urgent: Get rid of Reagan.

In the process, blacks hope to help return the Senate to Democratic control, strengthen the Democratic majority in the House, elect more blacks as mayors, judges and state legislators, and support white liberals and moderates.

The high point prior to this year's elections was the 1976 election of Jimmy Carter. Nearly 85 percent of the black vote went to Carter, and blacks took credit for providing the margin of victory. Carter acknowledged the pivotal role played by blacks, and showed his appreciation by appointments to his Administration and the judiciary.

Mrs. Austin points out that black political activity did not begin with Jackson, and she is echoed by others, including Eddie N. Williams, president of the Joint Center for Political Studies. Seeking political power, Williams says, was a natural consequence of the civil-rights movement. Fueling that is the discontent of many blacks who have not fared as well as expected economically.

"The election of conservatives changed the Government," Williams says. "Their agenda was to reduce Government participation, fight inflation and not to enforce rights laws. That plus the recession shut off the flow to economic empowerment. Blacks reacted by turning more to politics. With major victories in numerous places, the attitude became, 'We can do it,' or as Jesse Jackson said, 'It's our time.'

"Blacks believe they have the numbers. They were being ignored and felt their backs were against the wall. Therefore, they felt they had to come out and vote and be politically active. The alternative was to throw bricks."

To fire up the troops, black leaders are pounding away at the fact that President Reagan's margins of victory in New York, Mississippi, Alabama, Louisiana, Tennessee, South Carolina, North Carolina, Arkansas, Massachusetts, Kentucky and Virginia were less than the number of unregistered blacks in each state. In New York, for example, Reagan beat Jimmy Carter by 165, 459 votes. If the approximately 900,000 unregistered blacks in New York had registered and voted, the outcome probably would have been different.

Many blacks believe the recognition of their growing voting strength has already produced a change in both the Democratic and Republican parties. The recent bill to make the birthday of Martin Luther King Jr. a national holiday, for example, drew the support of both conservative Democrats and Republicans in Congress—and passed. Such conservative Republicans as Senator Strom Thurmond of South Carolina, a former segregationist whose 1957 filibuster against civil-rights legislation was the longest in history, have begun openly to court black voters.

The emergence of the black vote as a formidable power seems all the more significant after two losses last year: Los Angeles's Mayor Tom Bradley in the California Governor's race and Mississippi's State Senator Robert Clark in a Congressional contest. Bradley lost by fewer than 50,000 votes. The pall cast over blacks by those defeats has been replaced by a determination to work harder. Harold Washington's upset victory in Chicago this year and subsequent mayoral victories had a rejuvenating effect and have contributed to the current optimism and the candidacy of Jackson, a key backer of Chicago's new Mayor.

One of the most effective registration efforts under way is in Atlanta, a city with a history of black political participation and strength. The city's liberal tradition has helped develop a sophisticated black political system not duplicated elsewhere in the South, and few places in the North. Although an alliance of black Democrats and Republicans once guided the political fortunes of black Atlantans, the city is now run by the Democrats.

The registration campaign in Atlanta maintains a semblance of bipartisanship, but the anti-Reagan fervor among blacks is a constant that Democrats have a hard time containing. The local N.A.A.C.P. runs the campaign from its new single-story office building on Fairburn Road in a quiet wooded section. One of its small rooms has the character of a war room, as, indeed, it is—in a war against the Reagan Administration.

Of the 283,884 residents registered in Fulton County, 122,408 are black, leaving 78,972 blacks unregistered. "We want to get 50, 000 of the unregistered on the rolls by next year," says Jondelle Johnson, N.A.A.C.P. branch executive director.

Mrs. Johnson is a former journalist and a community activist with a reputation as an excellent organizer. Twenty years ago, she helped found The Atlanta Inquirer as an alternative to the Atlanta Daily World, a conservative local black daily that was opposed to the civil-rights movement.

"We've registered 10,000 people since June 1," she says. "We conduct a drive year round, not just on special occasions. We're the umbrella organization under which other groups work." Other groups involved are fraternal societies, block associations and churches.

She switched on the lights in the room to reveal an elaborate neighborhood canvassing system that uses maps of Atlanta and Fulton County, charts and graphs and rosters of names. On one wall, pins flagged with the number of voters registered dotted a map outlining census tracts. Armed with these tracts, 900 block captains canvass their neighborhoods, giving residents registration kits, telling them where they can vote and driving them to the polls if necessary. Georgia changed its law to allow registration at such places as K-Mart, Food Giant and Majik Market.

"Our plan is to find those unregistered people and get them on the rolls," says Mrs. Johnson. "There are three phases of our drive: an intensive campaign that goes till Dec. 31; another one in the spring for the primary, and then for the general election next November."

The N.A.A.C.P.'s campaign includes outdoor billboards and posters on buses and trains. Constant reminders on black radio stations also get the word out, and emphasize the importance of this medium in the black community. Radio was given special credit for the success in Chicago of Harold Washington, who, unlike former Mayor Jane Byrne and others, could not afford an expensive television blitz.

A jamboree of jazz and popular music planned for December is expected to attract young Atlantans, who must show proof of registration to gain admission. Registration also will be conducted on the spot, says Mrs. Johnson.

The elements of the increasingly intensive campaign going on in Atlanta and elsewhere are varied. In many places, voter registration and education campaigns are tied to electing black candidates to high-visibility offices. Before Edward M. McIntyre entered the race for Mayor of Augusta four years ago, he told black residents they would have to register if they wanted him to run. They did, and elected him the city's first black Mayor. The registration campaign in Charlotte, N.C., succeeded in making Harvey Gantt that city's first black Mayor.

In Miami this month, bloc voting by blacks was said to have been one major element in the election of Maurice A. Ferre, a moderate Democrat, to a sixth term as Mayor. In Boston, black participation did not appear to be a main factor in the record-level turnout at the mayoral elections, but Melvin King garnered an estimated 20 percent of the white vote. In the aftermath, his white opponent, Raymond L. Flynn, donned a rainbow coalition button at victory ceremonies. J. D. Nelson, King's campaign chairman, commented: "We've accomplished a lot in Boston. A minority candidate will always be taken seriously in this city from now on."

The highly organized and effective registration campaigns, conducted nationally and locally, hope to produce more victories. Operation Big Vote in Washington oversees the national effort, providing advice to local leaders conducting registration drives. The operation is nonpartisan and sponsored by the National Coalition on Black Voter Participation, which comprises various national and regional groups. The Republican National Committee, for example, and other groups each pay an annual membership fee of $250 to participate in the coalition. Some black Republicans feel their party is cutting its own throat by helping to register a group that is likely to vote overwhelmingly for Democrats.

The local campaigns appear to be attracting a good number of the young as volunteers. They were the foot soldiers of the re-election campaigns in Augusta and Birmingham, where Richard Arrington recently won a second term as Mayor. Leaders, expecting more to sign on next year, are aiming programs expressly at the young, who have the worst voting record of any segment of the electorate. The N.A.A.C.P. reported that during a 360-mile "over-ground railroad" march from Covington, Ky., to Detroit that it staged last summer, and which was led by its executive director, Benjamin L. Hooks, many of the 5,000 new voters enlisted were young people.

Recently, formal and informal conferences on the local and national level have helped rally blacks around the issues. The annual Congressional Black Caucus Weekend last September and a special meeting called last summer by the National Black Conference of Locally Elected Officials both discussed broad political issues. New Jersey blacks held a similar conference last summer. As part of an effort to defeat Mayor Koch in the next election, New York City blacks have held conventions the last two summers. The Coalition for a Just New York has begun a voter-registration drive whose slogan is "Strive for '85."

That the Democratic Party will be the beneficiary of most of the registration and politicization is almost universally accepted. Blacks have been the party's most consistent constituency, casting 20 to 22 percent of the Democratic vote total in the last four Presidential elections—making them more loyal than Jews, ethnic Catholics, Hispanics or Southern whites.

"Two things Democratic candidates must realize," says Williams of the Joint Center for Political Studies. "They must come by the black community in the primaries and again in the general election, and the Democrats can't win without a strong black vote."

Most black leaders agree. Black numerical strength is apparent throughout the country, particularly in the key industrial states of New York, New Jersey, Illinois, Ohio, Michigan and Pennsylvania. According to a Joint Center study analyzing the black vote, "No presidential candidate since Dwight Eisenhower in 1952 has won the Presidency without winning at least three of these six states. In a closely contested election, a cohesive black vote can easily be decisive in all of them."

"The 1982 election was the first post-Reagan election and was a good example of the power of the black vote," comments Eddie Williams. "Blacks elected four new black members of the House; they were the determining factor in several state elections, including the gubernatorial races in New York and Texas; they defeated three conservative Republican Congressmen, and helped several moderate Congressmen retain their seats."

The center's study concluded that the off-year election was, in effect, a referendum on President Reagan. Polls, including one by The New York Times/CBS News, also showed that blacks were less willing than whites to be patient with the Administration and give its programs a chance.

"Because many whites were sympathetic to Reagan's stated goals in the abstract, but were troubled by the concrete evidence that his policies were producing economic hardship," wrote Thomas E. Cavanagh, a research associate at the Joint Center and the author of the study, "many whites appear to have reserved judgment on Reagan's policies and cast their votes primarily on other grounds, while blacks considered both themselves and the country in jeopardy from Reagan's policies, and therefore voted Democratic.

"With over seven million voting-age blacks remaining unregistered, the addition of up to two million additional black voters to the registration rolls would appear to be a realistic possibility."

The target next year is not only President Reagan, but a number of Senate Republicans, including Thurmond, Jesse Helms of North Carolina and Thad Cochran of Mississippi. Blacks also hope to play a leading role in determining the outcome in Senate races in Tennessee and Texas, where Senate Majority Leader Howard H. Baker Jr. and John Tower, respectively, are retiring. Other Republicans, like Senator Charles Percy of Illinois, who otherwise have good civil-rights records, might be victims of the anti-Reagan sentiment.

Fingering his glass of Scotch in the Palm Tavern, Conrad Worrill, a history professor at Northeastern Illinois University's Center for Inner Cities Studies, reminisced about his participation in Harold Washington's Chicago mayoral campaign. He and the tavern's owner, Gerri Oliver, recalled the brief moment of renewed glory the campaign brought East 47th Street, a thoroughfare of dilapidated buildings separating the well-ordered lawns of Hyde Park from some of Chicago's worst slums. The tavern, across the street from the somber brick building that was Washington's campaign headquarters, served as the watering hole for workers and the place to celebrate the upset victory last April.

For Worrill, a militant, the excitement of the last campaign is gone, and Washington is now several miles away in City Hall, where he has become embroiled in a power struggle with the City Council's white majority. But with the Presidential primary season approaching and Jesse Jackson's candidacy announced, his · juices are flowing again. Worrill supports Jackson.

Jackson's entry into the race for the Presidency has, so far, produced mixed results. Rank-and-file blacks identify with Jackson, and his charismatic preachings have attracted a strong following. While many of them are excited, black leaders remain less than enthusiastic; in private, a few are hostile.

Prior to announcing his decision to run, the Baptist preacher traversed the country for months delivering his message of: "Power. Vote. Run. If you run, you may lose, but if you don't run you're guaranteed to lose." He coupled that theme with a constant drumbeat against the Reagan Administration. Even some of his critics give him credit for whipping up anti-Reagan sentiment and for inspiring blacks to register.

However, some black politicians like Atlanta Councilman John Lewis, a veteran civil-rights leader, openly question Jackson's motives in seeking the Presidency. Lewis says the black electorate doesn't want to be part of a symbolic effort, which he believes the Jackson candidacy is, despite assurances from Jackson that he is after the nomination. "The greater need is to see changes in the White House and Congress," says Lewis, "and we can't do that with a symbolic candidate. We've got to coalesce with others who share our concerns and make a majority of that coalition next year."

Jackson himself speaks of forming a "rainbow coalition" to take on Ronald Reagan and the Republicans. He says his aim in seeking the Presidency is to change the nature of national politics so it "will include the disaffected, those who have been denied inclusion in the process—blacks, women, Hispanics, native Americans—a new coalition of Americans, a new coalition of leadership."

Yet many blacks, including Eddie Williams, dismiss the notion of coalition politics as not only unrealistic but unnecessary at this time. One black leader asserts that too many differences—experience, background and language chief among them—stand between the two groups. "Nobody wants to be a junior partner in a relationship," he says, "and blacks have been that for too long in the Democratic Party."

Many blacks have serious problems with Jackson, and they boil down to mistrust. Some leaders and many middle-class blacks see Jackson as an egotistical publicity seeker and self-promoter, even a demagogue. Many believe Jackson's effort will unnecessarily divide the black community and that he is seizing the opportunity to succeed Martin Luther King Jr. as the premier black spokesman.

Jackson is widely regarded as a leader who marches to his own tune, and he has acknowledged as much. While he sees nothing wrong with his independent style, others complain that it gives him a blank check to do what he wants. "I wouldn't want Jesse acting as my broker at the Democratic convention," one prominent black leader says.

Georgia State Senator Julian Bond says: "Jesse will get support from a lot of local blacks who don't particularly like him or his style, but who see such support as helping their own causes and ambitions. I know a city councilman in California who privately can't stand Jesse, but publicly is for him because Jesse's popularity enhances the councilman's standing with his constituency. The councilman also feels that Jesse will help increase voter participation. There are a lot of people around the country in that position.

"And it is a mutual thing," Bond adds. "Jesse is getting their support, whether they like him or not. And they are getting his. But they haven't thought beyond the present to what Jesse's running means down the line, taking time, effort and money away from the primary goal, getting rid of Reagan.

"I am concerned that the registration effort could be undermined if many of those blacks that we register between now and next year don't go to the polls out of disappointment and frustration after Jesse's campaign ends."

Williams says that is a real possibility, but it would depend on how Jackson reacted to the loss of the nomination that few observers feel he has a chance of winning. If he is publicly bitter, many blacks might stay away from the polls. But, Williams says, if Jackson "is the statesman, if he puts the face of victory on whatever happens, if he leads the charge, it should inspire people to vote."

Those concerned that Jackson might be a spoiler recall the defeat of Hubert H. Humphrey, the 1968 Democratic Presidential candidate, after many of the embittered supporters of Eugene McCarthy and other Democrats did not vote or supported other candidates, allowing Richard Nixon to win by a narrow margin. Jackson, who dismisses this argument, claims his candidacy will only bring in more new voters for the Democrats.

Bond, who has endorsed Walter F. Mondale's candidacy, is concerned that if the other candidates in the primaries "let Jesse have the black vote, we've got to lose in the end because the winner is going to be one of the white guys, and he will have won without the help of blacks. There would be nothing for us. Jesse's risking removing blacks from the Democratic camp."

Jackson's track record, many complain, is long on rhetoric and short on accomplishment. Some feel his Operation People United to Serve Humanity (PUSH), with its national network of ministers, does little more than serve Jackson's interests. Jackson is also considered a poor administrator, inept at dealing with details and completing tasks. He denies most of the charges, declaring that he is a gadfly whose purpose is to inspire others.

"My talent is to motivate people," Jackson says, "to get them moving and acting to solve problems. I don't have to stick around, for example, to personally register everyone who needs registering. If I get a registration drive off to a good start, then it's up to somebody else to carry it through. That's my role."

Jackson, who once said he would not run until he had "the money, the machinery and the masses in place," is still in the process of building his campaign organization. And his recent fund-raising efforts have literally resembled the old Baptist technique of passing the collection plate. He recently appointed Arnold Pinkney, a deputy director of the 1972 Presidential campaign of Hubert H. Humphrey and now a partner in a Cleveland insurance agency, national director of his campaign. Pinkney, a key field organizer in Ohio for President Carter's re-election campaign in 1980, ran two successful re-election campaigns for Representative Louis Stokes. He was also minority director of Richard F. Celeste's successful 1982 Ohio gubernatorial campaign.

Jackson carries into the race the antagonism of many Jews, based on his 1979 visit with leaders of other black organizations to Lebanon. Press accounts included a photograph of Jackson embracing Yasir Arafat, head of the Palestine Liberation Organization. This month, Jackson met with the American Israel Public Affairs Committee in Washington in an attempt to improve understanding. So far, however, Jews are conspicuously absent from his rainbow coalition.

Jackson's penchant for unpredictable behavior can have an alienating effect. His trip to Europe last summer was, for many, an irritating example. In London, he announced an impromptu plan for a petition drive for 100 million signatures calling for South Africa to end apartheid. When pressed about who would organize and pay for such a drive, he suggested the peace movement, a suggestion promptly rejected by some of its leaders. In the Netherlands, he undiplomatically repeated to the press his conversation with Queen Beatrix. In West Berlin, he failed to show up for breakfast with the Lord Mayor.

His late and long-awaited announcement to seek the Presidential nomination was vintage Jackson. After setting a news conference for Nov. 3, Jackson scooped himself on CBS News's "60 Minutes" four days beforehand. This incident left a sour taste among many in the press and within his own staff.

Such erratic behavior notwithstanding, even his critics agree that Jackson should do well among blacks. Many agree that his presence in certain primaries will rouse more blacks to register and go to the polls to vote. As a result, more blacks could win local offices.

Yet many blacks fear that Mondale, the white candidate most attractive to blacks, will be the loser. Mondale would certainly lose black votes to Jackson, possibly enabling the more conservative John Glenn, the Ohio Senator, to gain the nomination.

Not surprisingly, Charles Smith, a black political aide to Glenn, welcomes Jackson's candidacy. "We talk and are helpful to the Jackson campaign workers," he says. "We share our expertise with them and help them with logistics."

Already in his campaign, Jackson has provoked fear among some Democrats. He refused to rule out running as an independent in next year's general election, holding that as an option should he lose the nomination. It is an option that might guarantee President Reagan's re-election.

Jackson is in a unique position. Although he is virtually certain to lose his bid for the Democratic nomination, he can use his candidacy not only to enunciate issues affecting blacks, women and poor people but also to raise broader questions about American priorities and involvements nationally and internationally.

"This nation needs a new industrial policy," Jackson says. "Workers must share in policy making, profits and risks.

"We can't allow the corporations to take our tax dollars and put dioxin in the earth and pollute the ground. They use cheap labor in Taiwan and South Korea. Reagan gives our jobs to robots and slaves. There must be a new industrial policy."

Many blacks, their reservations about Jackson aside, see his candidacy for the nation's highest office as a well-timed and galvanizing symbol for all blacks. Still, Jackson, who skillfully challenges his audiences to get involved in the political process, risks much if he cannot direct those energies to the polling booth.

Clearly, blacks have rediscovered the power of the ballot, and they are being wooed in turn by Democratic and Republican office seekers. Any gains will ultimately depend on how many follow through and actually vote. Although other elections are forthcoming, the major test of that power will come in November 1984.

WHAT'S NEXT?[2]

It was ninety-five years ago when Frederick Douglass received a single vote at the 1888 Republican convention in Chicago, making him the first black to receive such attention from a major political party. Douglass recorded another such first as well; sixteen years earlier, in 1872, he was nominated in absentia for vice president by the newly-formed Equal Rights Party. The presidential nominee was Victoria Woodhull, a suffragist.

[2]Reprint of a speech delivered by Julian Bond, Georgia State Senator, at the Association for the Study of Afro-American Life and History annual meeting, October 20, 1983. Reprinted from *Negro History Bulletin*. 46:72+. Jl. Ag. S. '83. Copyright © 1983 by the Association for the Study of Afro-American Life and History, Incorporated, 1401 14th Street, N. W., Washington, D. C. 20005.

Douglass was chosen because of his reputation, and because he was black. Symbolism was important, even then.

"We have the oppressed sex represented by Woodhull," said the man who nominated him. "We must have the oppressed race represented by Douglass."

Douglass declined the nomination. Ulysses S. Grant was nominated by the Republicans, Horace Greeley by the Democrats, and Grant won.

One hundred eleven years later, no issue has divided America's black political community as much as the question of whether—and if so, with whom—blacks ought to once again contest the presidency in next year's Democratic primaries.

Former friends have become instant enemies as they dig in and settle down on various sides of this debate.

Nominal allies have become at least temporary opponents as the benefits and dangers of running and not running are argued with at least as much heat as light.

The question takes on a special urgency because of what is at stake next year—not electing a black person president, but rejecting the president who is and has been more hostile to our concerns than any other.

For three years we have lived under an administration run by an amiable incompetent, the architect of avarice and social policy.

When he first took office, we were fearful—today we know what real fear is.

Then, we thought our civil rights were in jeopardy—today we see them swiftly slipping away.

Then, Reaganomics was an unproved economic theory—today it remains an unproved theory, but its application threatens to make the depression look like a Sunday school picnic.

From Buffalo to Gary, the United States is in its worst depression in 50 years. Plants are closed daily, shifts are laid off.

Eighty-eight percent of black youth are jobless in Gary; 83 percent in Riverside, California; 80 percent in Youngstown, Ohio; and 70 percent in Montgomery, Alabama.

By mid-summer, 100,000 young people in New York City had become discouraged workers—abandoning the search for jobs in a society which has abandoned them. Ten percent of our total work force is idle. Thirty percent of our manufacturers' capacity is at rest. Fifty-seven cents of every federal tax dollar is committed to militarily-related expenses. Two-thirds of the interest payments on the national debt are war-related. Our government opposes abortion, and supports the death penalty—they believe life begins at conception and ends at birth.

They intend to rearrange America to fit their sterile vision, to force conformity with their small minds and smaller dreams. Riding the crest of a wave of antagonism against those Americans who cannot do for themselves, they intend to impose an awful austerity on us all. This conservative confederacy intends as well to take the federal government entirely out of the business of enforcing equal opportunity in America.

They intend to eliminate affirmative action for women and minorities.

They intend to erase the laws and programs written in blood and sweat in the 20 years since Martin Luther King was the premier figure in black America, and black America seemed single-minded in pursuit of its freedom.

We have done more than change the name of the occupant of the oval office, the face in the photograph on the post office wall. The election began the process of marching America backward into the 18th century, and surrendered our foreign policy to men who believe that all national struggles for self-determination are directed from Moscow and that nuclear war is a viable option.

At home—and abroad—they have surrendered the general good to the corporate will. They intend to radically alter the relationship between America and Africa, to substitute mineral rights for human rights, and have already begun to embrace and endorse the most horrific government on the face of the planet earth. Their favored allies and models in the world community are clients and tyrants.

They prefer the hardware of war to the handiworks of peace.

They are the first American government in two decades to use food as an aggressive weapon, to add starvation to the American arsenal.

They support workers' movements in Warsaw and crush them in Washington. They intend, in fact, to use the power of government to further consolidate wealth in the minority of our population, to redistribute income from the bottom to the top, to undermine the Bill of Rights, to re-introduce big brother to the American scene.

The Reagan Administration has begun an aggressive campaign to dismantle and dissolve the civil rights protections written into law over the last 25 years. To the President and the Attorney General, the Constitution is a document of almost infinite elasticity, to be cut and snipped to suit the fashion of the moment. They intend, in fact, to turn back the civil rights clock until it becomes a sundial.

For the Reagan Administration, equal opportunity means a better than even chance for minorities and women to be unemployed. It means an unequal chance at the welfare rolls, a head start in hopelessness, and affirmation of the opportunity America has always guaranteed blacks to be last hired and first fired. This assault on civil rights is coupled with an all-out attack on the yet unfulfilled right of every American to be free of want and economic worry. Millions of families, poor and working poor, are being herded further into poverty as they slip through a safety net so fragile a minnow would escape, so porous it could not contain Moby Dick.

A study conducted by a former Nixon Administration official for the University of Chicago Center for the Study of Welfare Policy concluded:

"The effects of the Reagan proposals will be to drive many low-income families deeper into poverty while inflation continues to deplete the value of their diminishing incomes, and to shift significant fiscal administrative and political burdens onto states and localities whose budgets are already in the red. The President claims that he will leave a 'safety net' intact to protect low-income Americans. This is simply not so."

The fact that one-third of all American families will be negatively affected by the Reagan cuts is a clear reminder of the necessity for a continuing struggle to end economic discrimination in the United States; that disproportionate numbers of these families are black or brown is an unnecessary reminder that white supremacy remains an essential feature of the culture of mainstream America and may be permanently rooted in the American character.

The President's policies, in sum, are anti-family and anti-black.

The promise that each American would bear an equal burden is as empty as the pockets of our ten million unemployed. As the destruction of the social safety net has moved forward, and as the human infrastructure of America begins to collapse under a deliberate design of calculated neglect, the greedy appetite of the military machine grows more voracious every day. The administration is beating our plowshares into swords and our pruning hooks into spears. The choice they put before us is greater than guns versus butter; it is soup kitchens and surplus cheese versus expensive airplanes and malfunctioning tanks.

Between the day he took the oath of office and 1988, President Reagan is asking you to spend $1.996 trillion dollars on defense. This is enough money—as if you had spent $1 billion dollars a year since Jesus was born—to give every American alive today $7,000.00—to finance World War II and two years of the Social Security program, or—to build a stack of $1,000 bills 134 miles high.

We may all agree then, that our situation is desperate, and that Ronald Reagan's continuation in office five minutes past the expiration of his present term would be catastrophic for black people. To run, or not to run—that appears to be the question.

Before any final conclusions are reached, it may be well to have the facts before us, to examine closely the history of past attempts to put a black face in the White House or on a party ticket, to see whether or not the complicated arithmetic and rules of the Democratic Party's delegate selection process make such an attempt likely to return real benefits to all of black America.

That last point is absolutely essential—what is under discussion in most places today is an assault on the Democratic Party's nomination for the Presidency of the United States, and not an independent race for the White House.

Nonetheless, a June 5 Gallup Poll tells us that an independent race for president in 1984 by the Reverend Jesse Jackson against expected Republican nominee Ronald Reagan and possible Democratic nominee Walter Mondale would certainly and easily guarantee a Reagan victory.

It is important to note that Jackson has disavowed an independent candidacy, much as John Anderson did. He then ended his race for the Republican nomination and faced Jimmy Carter and Ronald Reagan as an independent in November, 1980.

Crusades are difficult to contain; constant celebrity almost impossible to abandon voluntarily.

The Gallup figures show that an independent Jackson candidacy in the November, 1984 general election would reduce Reagan's expected share of black votes from 10% of the total cast to 7%. Walter Mondale's expected 80% share of black votes would be reduced to only 29%, causing his defeat, and the Rev. Jackson would end in third place with 48% of black votes cast. Gallup's projections are that 41% of all voters would choose Reagan, giving him another four year lease on the Presidency and another four-year noose around black people's neck; Mondale would finish a close second, a position important only in horseshoes, with 40% of the total vote, and Rev. Jackson would come in last place with 9% of all votes cast. (Gallup Poll, June 5, 1983)

In this second scenario, Jackson's gains are again Mondale's losses, and while we may properly acknowledge that polls taken in early June of 1983 may have little relation to events which may transpire in November of 1984, it is safe to conclude that an independent black candidacy ought to be dismissed out of hand today, and attempts to breathe life into such a campaign next year attacked as the suicidal attempt such a race would surely be. Any political action whose chief effect is re-electing Ronald Reagan deserves the contempt of American black people.

Let us focus then instead on the probabilities and possibilities of a black candidate in next year's Democratic primaries and caucuses, on his or her chances to win sizeable numbers of delegates and to influence the selection of an eventual nominee and platform by the party.

Is anyone here talking of a black person winning the nomination or general election? If not, we may then proceed.

A May 1983 poll in the *Garth Analysis* showed Jackson running third for the Democratic nomination, with 9% of the Democratic vote. He placed third behind Mondale, who won with 36% of the Democratic vote, and John Glenn, who placed second with 24%.

Since blacks are as much as 20% of the total Democratic electorate, 9% of the total Democratic vote may not be encouraging. The *Garth Analysis* says that Jackson's candidacy would harm Mondale's chances, reducing Mondale's share of black votes from 48 to 21%. (*The Garth Analysis,* May, 1983)

The most recent poll taken before this meeting that I could discover—released in the August 29 issue of *Newsweek* magazine—confirmed the effects of a campaign by Rev. Jackson.

Newsweek says a Jackson campaign would reduce Reuben Askew's black vote by one percentage point, from 3 to 2%; Alan Cranston's share of black votes would be cut in half, from 4 to 2%; John Glenn's black vote would be cut from 15 to 9%; Gary Hart's one percent share of black votes would be totally erased, and Walter Mondale's commanding 47% of black votes would be reduced to 29%, the same figure as in the June Gallup Poll I cited earlier.

Only Ernest Hollins—to whom *Newsweek* gives a modest 2% of black votes—would be unaffected by Jesse Jackson entering the Democratic primary race.

Until this moment, all of the effects attributable in the least respect to the threat—real or actual—that a black person may contest the Presidency have been overwhelmingly positive.

Several thousand new black registrants have been added to the voters' roll, as quite probably will several thousands more. Most have been registered as the result of organized efforts by the traditional organizations like the NAACP; others have taken the initiative on their own, but all are motivated, at least in part, by the rush of excitement that has permeated black political activity recently.

The current increase in black voting strength interestingly predates our current concerns with candidates and presidential politics.

It surfaced first in the 1982 mid-term elections, when black voters recorded a gain in voting rates over 1978's Congressional contests at five times the increase recorded by Hispanics and twice the rates of increase for whites. In nine states, blacks voted at rates higher than whites, demonstrating that candidate color may be less important in stimulating the black electorate than had been supposed.

Increases continued in 1983, with the unprecedented registration and turnout in Harold Washington's victory in Chicago and carried forward through Wilson Goode's primary victory in Philadelphia and the unsuccessful William Murphy campaign in Baltimore.

When the possibility of a black presidential candidate is added to these more easily attainable goals, and when the real opportunity to reverse and erase four years of Reaganism presents itself next year, it is natural that interest in voting among the people who have seen the vote deliver real change would be heightened.

Indeed, if there are any lessons to be learned from the recent March on Washington for Jobs, Peace and Freedom, it is that black America remains convinced overwhelmingly of the efficacy of politics as a means of group advancement.

Not as the only means, surely, but speaker after speaker at that gathering exhorted the audience to correct the imbalance between white and black registration and voting rates, and to use the power of the ballot to right the wrongs done to us.

The announced Democratic candidates are surely more aware of the power of black votes—potential and actual—than in past campaigns.

In the past, we were often content to vote for candidates because they knew the words to our hymns; today's crop is competing for black votes on a slightly higher plane, offering issues and not emotions.

The incumbent, having deliberately alienated black voters in order to attract the sizeable portion of white supremacists in the general population, is now engaged in trying to win those voters whose skins are brown, and to avoid alienating those moderate whites who view with horror the administration's regressive civil rights policies.

Why then shouldn't some black person run for President again? Surely not simply to prove to our children that it can be done—Frederick Douglass proved that almost 100 years ago, and Mrs. Shirley Chisholm re-proved it in 1972. Others proved it before and since, giving ample testimony that a black person can run for President, as a Democrat, a Republican, or representative of practically any party. It has already been done. To suggest that doing it again in 1984 proves a point somehow unproven to date negates our history and cheapens our past struggles. That history is worth reviewing, briefly.

It isn't surprising that the history of efforts by blacks to be nominated by political parties large and small is so sketchy—black people weren't even invited to an inaugural ball until 1949.

If Douglass was the first black to receive a Presidential vote at a Republican convention, in 1888, the Rev. Channing Phillips of the District of Columbia seems to be the first black to get a vote at the Democratic convention, 80 years later in 1968. He received 67.5 votes. 1968 was notable because two other blacks ran for President that year as well—Dick Gregory as candidate of the New Party, and Eldridge Cleaver as nominee of the Peace and Freedom Party. Four years later, in 1972, former U.S. Representative Shirley Chisholm made what must be considered the best organized and best financed race to date for a major party's nomination.

She won 28 delegates and received 151.25 votes at the convention, losing to George McGovern.

With such a record of past efforts behind us, some other justification must be found today to rationalize what will be a great expenditure of material and human capital, and the enormous risks taken by the person who offers as candidate.

The risks are real, for personal and character assassination are realistic chances any presidential candidate, white or black, must assume.

When the candidate makes actual threats against the *status quo,* as any black candidate must do, the risks escalate.

Are the risks, then, equal to the prize? And if the prize isn't victory, then what can it be? How can success be measured in a race in which one contestant's supporters admit he won't reach the finish line and the main effect of his running at all will be to eliminate the next most favored candidate? The only answer must be the effect he will have on the other candidates.

However liberalized they may be by the threat of a black candidacy, none of the announced candidates for the Democratic nomination is as likely to represent black interests as candidate, nominee or President as a black person might. At best they are lighter shades of pale compared to the deep dark strength that the concentrated power of a disciplined and unified black electorate can bring to the Presidential nominating process next year. Understanding that process and the weight it gives to well-organized sectors of the electorate are crucial to weighing the chances of a black candidate next year.

Although the first contests of the 1984 Democratic Presidential selection process will be held on February 27, when Iowa opens its tiered system of selecting delegates in caucuses, and on March 6, when New Hampshire holds its primary, for blacks the race begins on March 13, when primaries are held in Alabama, Florida, and Georgia.

Although other primaries and caucuses are held in other states on that day, these three states have 15 Congressional districts between them in which a black candidate may be expected to do more than simply show up. Three days later, Mississippi and South Carolina Democrats will caucus; these two states have 11 districts between them where a black candidate may be reasonably expected to elect delegates.

Here is where an understanding of the rules is crucial. Each state is accorded a base delegation, $\frac{3}{4}$ths of which is elected by districts and $\frac{1}{4}$th at-large, and each state is given a 10% add-on, reserved for party and elected officials. All of these delegates must be pledged, must either publicly declare for a candidate or announce they are uncommitted.

Then each state receives another add-on of delegates, also reserved for party and elected officials. These delegates will be unpledged. Half of all delegates will be men.

As a general proposition, a Presidential candidate must receive 25% of the votes cast in a district; without that 25%, he fails to place at all. Only 86 of the United States' 435 Congressional districts have even a 20% or greater Black population.

It is clear then a Black candidate must win, and win well in those 86 districts, unless he or she can count on something neither Harold Washington nor Coleman Young nor Andrew Young nor Maynard Jackson nor Wilson Goode could—votes from a large minority of non-black voters.

You may know that the Joint Center for Political Studies has developed a "best case" scenario for a Black candidate in 1984. Their research suggests that 778 of the 3,923 delegates to the 1984 Democratic Convention in San Francisco can be black, and that as many as 250 of those delegates could be pledged to a black candidate. (Outlook For A Black Presidential Candidacy, the Joint Center for Political Studies, Washington, D.C., March 10, 1983)

The Joint Center sums up the risks as well.

As we have noted, one risk is drawing votes away from a candidate who, in the absence of the black candidate, would be the most attractive nominee to black voters.

In that same vein, overwhelming support for a black candidate who nonetheless does not receive enough delegate votes to block or influence the nomination leads inevitably to the selection of a white candidate chosen with little participation from black voters, and little reason to be responsive to their concerns.

There are other risks—suffice it to say that this process ought not be entered upon as cavalierly as has sometimes been true in the past, and it ought never to be thought of as the only course we can follow.

Our first black Presidential candidate, Frederick Douglass, described the course of action we must follow over 100 years ago. He said then:

"Let me give you a word of the history of reform, the whole history of the progress of human liberty shows that all concessions yet made to her august claims have been born of earnest struggles, and for the time being, putting all other tumults to silence, it must do this or do nothing. If there is no struggle, there is no progress. Those who profess to favor freedom and yet deprecate agitation are men who want crops without plowing up the ground, they want rain without thunder and lightning. They want the ocean without the awful roar of its many waters.

This struggle may be a moral one, or it may be a physical one, and it may be both moral and physical, but it must be a struggle. Power concedes nothing without a demand. It never has, and it never will. Find out just what any people will quietly submit to, and you have found out the exact measure of injustice and wrong which will be imposed upon them, and these will continue until they are resisted with either words or blows or both. The limits of tyrants are prescribed by the endurance of those whom they oppress. . . .

Men may not get all they pay for in this world, but they certainly must pay for all they get. If we ever get free from the oppressions and wrongs heaped upon us, we must pay for their removal. We must do this by labor, by suffering, by sacrifice, and if needs be, by our lives, and the lives of others."

BLACK POWER IN THE AGE OF JACKSON[3]

Black power is an engine that drives the great vehicles of social change in America. The Civil War and the civil rights movement, slave revolts and student sit-ins, Marcus Garvey's separatism and Malcolm X's nationalism: black people's epic struggle for equality and quest for identity create both the pretext and the context for national upheaval and transformation. It is a radical dynamic that pertains to America's peculiar racial history, and in each generation it produces unique politics and unexpected leaders. Suddenly, in this electoral season, the politics are Presidential and the leader is Jesse Jackson.

Both the man and the movement have caught America by surprise and have taken it by storm. The national media plaster Jackson's face on magazine covers, pull him in front of television cameras and tuck him into the most conventional categories of Presidential candidacy. Even the press that can't stand (or understand) his politics makes Jackson into some kind of hero; *Newsweek*'s cover story includes "a Jackson album" of snapshots, showing the candidate in historic poses from college football field to victory night after Chicago's mayoral election last winter. Not since John F. Kennedy burst into celebrity a quarter-century ago has a political upstart so captivated the press and captured attention, space and even *Time*: "He can be fascinating and frightening, inspiring and irritating, charismatic and controversial," the magazine intoned breathlessly.

Such effusions are accompanied by detailed analyses, often with charts, of the mathematical probabilities for Jackson's strategy to succeed in the primaries. Then come discussions of Jackson's

[3]Reprint of an article by associate editor Andrew Kopkind. *The Nation* 237:521+. N. 26, '83. Copyright © 1983, The Nation Associates.

stated or implied positions on what pundits take to be issues in the election: missiles, motherhood and the Palestine Liberation Organization, for three. Finally, Jackson albums usually include an extended essay by the resident philosopher on every black child's dream of becoming President of the United States.

The level of muddle, misinformation, wrong thinking and barely disguised racism in all the hoopla is extraordinary, if predictable. In listing Jackson's "downside," commentators invariably call him "ambitious," "egotistical," "opportunistic" and "driven," as if such qualities were rare among Presidential candidates. Who could be more ambitious than John Glenn, more opportunistic than Walter Mondale, more frightening than Ronald Reagan, more irritating than Gary Hart? But somehow (we *know* how) Jackson is fair game for taunts and teases from the press, while lighter folks get off with more qualified criticisms.

By the same token, the Jackson campaign and the phenomenon of a black political movement are consistently denigrated or trivialized. Many politicians see the surge of black activism as merely the latest minority bid for the spoils of office (and even that bespeaks a misreading of the history of ethnic politics); one leftish columnist said cynically, "The whole thing will end with Mondale making Jackson his Secretary of HUD, or something." I've heard it said that Jackson's purpose is to "keep the Democrats honest," an oxymoronic hope at best, or, along the same lines, to "revive the New Deal coalition," an improbable medical and political dream.

The cynics may have a point; they often do. The media may be able to frame the Jackson campaign in familiar terms of charisma, clout and the delegate count: those are the most comfortable clichés. Politicians may defang and defuse the frightening and explosive elements of the movement: that is their prerogative. But black politics in the Age of Jackson has a vastly different center of gravity, historical message and meaning. "It's all about power," Stoney Cooks, a longtime associate of Atlanta Mayor Andrew Young, told me recently. It's also about race, about class, about enfranchisement and disenfranchisement and about the mechanisms of change in the country. The movement is not peripheral to those transforming struggles in the American epic; it is at the very heart of the upheaval.

The sweep and pace are phenomenal. Jesse Jackson seems to be everywhere at once, commenting on everything, posing with everyone. Even before he announced his candidacy on November 3—in the week of Grenada and Lebanon—he was ranging wider than the other seven Democratic entrants combined: at the Berlin Wall, in The Hague, in Bonn and London, in a New York City armory for hearings on police brutality, at the Lincoln Memorial for the twentieth anniversary March on Washington, in the Waldorf Astoria for a gay rights dinner, in Bermuda for a meeting with a Salvadoran rebel leader, in remote New Hampshire getting visibility and in rural Mississippi getting potential voters to register.

Jackson's is the face at the front, but it is not the only representation of the quickening black movement. There are the triumphal images of Chicago's Mayor Harold Washington, Philadelphia's Mayor Wilson Goode and Boston's mayoral candidate Mel King; the demanding figures of the new local-hero politicians such as Brooklyn's Assemblyman Albert Vann and Representative Major Owens, Los Angeles's Assemblywoman Maxine Waters and Gary, Indiana's, Mayor Richard Hatcher—the granddaddy of the New Breed; the suggestive sight of caravans rumbling through Southern hamlets and Northern ghettos on voter registration drives. There is a rush of new symbols: a black Miss America, a black police commissioner for New York City, a black astronaut. The images become blurred as the old-guard leadership races to join the bandwagon. In the course of a few months everything has moved: the spirit is impatient, the mood is militant, the tempo is rising and the color is black.

The speed of change is unprecedented. At this time last year, black politicians and black politics were nearly invisible in white America. The decline of the old civil rights movement, the force of the white backlash to integration and affirmative action, and the rise of Reaganism had pushed black struggles into an Orwellian memory hole. Only two years ago, Adam Clymer, a senior political analyst for *The New York Times,* surveyed the scene and discovered that "the political influence of blacks in America has fallen to its lowest level in two decades."

The gains blacks had made in employment, education and political office after passage of the various antidiscrimination acts of the 1960s proved to be limited, and by the end of the next decade many of the vectors of progress were reversed. A report issued this year by the Center for the Study of Social Policy, a liberal think tank, showed that the median income for blacks was only 56 percent of that for whites—virtually the same as it was in 1960. Even worse, 45 percent of all adult black males were unemployed in 1982—almost twice as many as in 1960, also a year of economic downturn. Politically, black officeholders are still a token presence, even in Southern states with large black populations. There are no blacks among the eighty-two members of Congress from the seven states of the Deep South, where the Voting Rights Act of 1965 was targeted. As Jesse Jackson says repeatedly in his stump speeches, "Eighteen years after the Voting Rights Act, only 1 percent of elected officials are black. At that rate, it will take us 198 years to achieve parity."

Social relations between blacks and whites had been similarly stymied, if they had not actually deteriorated by the mid-1970s. Racist chic replaced radical chic (if the latter was ever anything more than a gonzo magazine headline); liberal guilt ebbed and liberal good will dissipated. Liberal malice, on the other hand, became socially legitimate and politically shrewd. New York's Mayor Ed Koch who once marched for black equality in Dixie runs from it like the plague in his own hometown, and there are other politicians like him. The elaborate coded vocabulary used to disguise the racist ethic they promote fools none but the most gullible editorial writers. Black and white voters (and nonvoters) know how to translate "death penalty," "victims' rights," "poverty pimps," "welfare cheats" and "special interests" when used in white political parlance. And they act accordingly on election day. All during the 1970s, whites voted for whites and many blacks didn't bother.

Things started changing a year ago. The black political movement arose from the cynicism, disillusionment and reaction of the last long years; indeed, the movement was fashioned by the despair of the decade following the demise of the civil rights campaigns. It appeared not only *after* that time of hopelessness, of rejection, of broken promises and false starts but *because* of the many failures. That is crucial for the movement, and for Jesse Jackson as well.

Both Jackson and the movement exploded into political prominence and media visibility during the Chicago mayoral campaign of Harold Washington. That contest became the pivotal event in the development of the new black consciousness, what Jackson calls the beginning of "a six-week drama around the [Washington] victory and a six-month trauma afterward." It was vastly different from other black electoral victories of the past fifteen years because it was won in direct opposition to—and at the expense of—white Democrats of the liberal persuasion.

Walter Mondale and Edward Kennedy, the diarchs of Democratic liberalism, came to Chicago to stump for Washington's opponents: Kennedy for incumbent Mayor Jane Byrne, Mondale for Richard M. Daley, son of the late cloutish Mayor. They hardly took notice of Washington's presence or his point, which was that it was black people's "turn" to hold office. The white politicians simply assumed what all white Democrats have assumed since the New Deal: blacks would be satisfied with the leavings of liberal power—the trickle down effects of welfare policies and expanded public employment programs. As it turned out, those assumptions were obsolete.

"Mondale and Kennedy came to Chicago to beat Harold Washington," Jackson remarked to me one steamy morning late last summer in a van bouncing through backwater Mississippi on a voter registration weekend. "You couldn't pay them to do that again. Things have changed."

What happened in Chicago was the beginning of the process Jackson calls the "renegotiation" of the relationship between blacks and the Democratic Party. For half a century, the Democrats have in a sense contracted to provide for and protect blacks and others traditionally rejected by the American system. Blacks were to respond with votes, support, enthusiasm and, perhaps most important, moral legitimacy. "Black voting is always sort of a moral initiative," Jackson said in a speech not long ago.

As the contract has run its course through several renewals but no serious reconstructions, the Democrats have often tried to wrig-

gle out of important clauses. Even the great New Dealer Franklin
Roosevelt was lambasted by black leaders for his poor performance; many did not want to support his campaign for a third
term. Kennedy fudged on civil rights until the movement overtook
him; organizers of the 1963 March on Washington were so suspi-
cious of his motives and wary of his rhetoric that they rejected his
request to speak at the Lincoln Memorial.

Lyndon Johnson wanted to be remembered for saying "We
shall overcome" at a joint session of Congress; but before that, as
he prepared for his nomination at the 1964 Democratic National
Convention in Atlantic City, he ordered the destruction of the
most important independent black political movement of that era,
the Mississippi Freedom Democratic Party. It's a long and sad
tale, but the upshot is that Johnson and Hubert Humphrey de-
manded that blacks give up any hope of independent political
standing and submit to the priorities, needs and strategies of white
Democratic leaders if they wanted antipoverty and civil rights
benefits.

Most whites forgot the Freedom Democrats' challenge soon
after the convention. But black activists and political workers—
including everyone I met at the heart of the Jackson campaign—
remember it vividly. For them, it is the landmark event in the development of black power consciousness and its political expression.

Everything Jesse Jackson is saying this year about blacks in
politics—"We want our share," "It's our turn," "Blacks will no
longer be the Harlem Globetrotters of the Democratic
Party"—was first shouted, in many of the same words, by young
black civil rights workers and militants in the wake of the liberal
"betrayal" of the Freedom Democrats. I heard the basic Jackson
in 1966 in Mississippi, when the first cries of "black power" went
up; in Lowndes County, Alabama, where members of the Student
Nonviolent Coordinating Committee settled down to start the
Black Panther Party; in Oakland, California, where other black
youths were organizing a similar project in an urban ghetto.

In all those cases, black power politics was the specific response to Democratic failures to give organized blacks a share in
the power and profits of political control. But as a slogan and an

idea, black power is old hat. Why has it taken nearly two decades for it to find expression in mainstream politics?

Jackson told me that blacks had to develop a certain amount of "maturity" before they could assimilate black power concepts and act on them. That means, perhaps, that they had to hear Democratic promises of provision and protection, believe them and see them broken. In other words, they had to want the Great Society and see it destroyed by the Democrats' war in Vietnam; they had to suffer the depredations of corporate conservatism under Nixon; they had to plead for a better deal from Carter and see that hope deferred by the exigencies of Democratic inflation-fighting and cold-warmongering, and they had to bear the brunt of Reaganism's ravages, unaided and hardly comforted by their Democratic protectors. It's no wonder that, in Chicago, blacks refused en masse to follow Mondale and Kennedy and give their votes, or their moral approval, to the white establishment which had led them on and let them down so many times.

To follow the political logic of black power politics is easier than to chart its future. But to see what the result of renegotiation may mean, it is best to start with Jesse Jackson's concept of black voting as a moral initiative. That view is surely more than bluff and pride. Black political activity has a unique potential in the American electoral scheme as a strategy in the struggle for justice and equality. That is not to say black votes count for more than those of any other group, but the fact of racism and the history of black exclusion give black electoral movements a special spiritual force.

A corollary to the formulation of moral initiative is Jackson's notion, which he explained to a New York audience recently, that "most other groups ride on the coattail of black strategy." That is not an altogether endearing insight: scores of self-perceived or self-constructed voting communities pretend to pre-eminence, not to mention political leadership. Whites of all stripes have historically ignored blacks and dismissed race as irrelevant or dangerous in political organization. Leftists sometimes call race mere "superstructure" over a class and economic fundament—an ideological maneuver that allows them to support whites against blacks in hopes of mobilizing the working-class racist vote for an economic "populist." Many liberals will plead "color blindness" at election time in order to preserve the myth of democratic equality. Most people, of course, simply shut race out of their mind when not actively expressing contempt or practicing violence against the nearest minority target. But because racism is a paradigm for every other ideology of exclusion, campaigns to combat it—black political campaigns—can provide an example for every other struggle in the system.

Jackson's "rainbow coalition" is an attempt to organize the political strength of all deprived and rejected constituencies around the moral force and political energy of the black movement. It is no gimmick, and although Jackson may throw the term around too breezily, he is deadly serious about it. It is the essence of his campaign.

"The civil rights movement . . . laid the foundations, provided the climate and in many instances trained the initial organizers of the women's, gay, antinuclear, environmental and other movements of the seventies and eighties," he told the audience at the gay Human Rights Campaign Fund dinner in New York. "Discrimination, oppression and on occasion genocide have been used to force blacks, women and Native Americans into their proper place. All of us feel deprived in twentieth-century America, and America is still organized by cash—the cash system that is still dominated by white males."

The political demands of the rainbow coalition, implicit in its construction and explicit in Jackson's speeches, are extraordinary. They are racial, sexual, economic and ideological. What other major-party candidate in this century has talked about deprivation in a "cash system dominated by white males"? No wonder Jackson is scaring conventional politicians half to death.

Bruce Bolling, Boston's black City Councilor, told a reporter last spring that Jackson "may be viewed as threatening. He's talking about a coalition of people on the outside, and in some quarters people might be anxious about that kind of direction."

It is enormously difficult to convince even a fraction of the "people on the outside" that their interests lie in political coalition, and even harder to talk them all into accepting black leadership—much less Jesse Jackson. And yet it makes perfect sense. The

Democrats understand it, but their coalitions have always served the purposes of the white male cash system. Jackson's campaign would establish an opposition to that dominance.

For its part, the Democratic Party leadership seems to have given up on opposition. It has supported Reagan in his imperial invasions; it has grown silent in the face of the business recovery; it has adopted "neoliberal" prejudices against labor, the poor, social welfare and economic redistribution. It is left to Jesse Jackson to stake out opposition ground on Grenada and Lebanon, for instance, on the nuclear arms race and corporate accountability and racial equity. It would hardly be an election campaign without him.

It should be said, although it hardly needs saying, that the contradictions in his candidacy and in the black political movement are heavy enough to bring the whole thing down at any time with just a little shoving. There will be plenty of that. Jackson's personality, background, faults and foibles will be excruciatingly exploited. He is so far out of the mold of the typical political candidate that almost everything he ever said or did, or says or does, can be used to invalidate his effort. Is the bookkeeping at PUSH (his Chicago-based organization, People United to Serve Humanity) messy? Did he say the wrong thing on abortion? Did he offend Jews, social democrats, environmentalists, lesbians? Probably. He makes a lot of mistakes, even in his own terms. But until now, at least, he has not been crafting a serious bid for the Presidency, and he has not stopped along the way to think that everything can, and will, be used against him.

"America rejects and excludes more people than it accepts and includes," Jackson said in announcing his candidacy. On paper, the rainbow coalition easily constitutes the "new majority" Jackson proposes. But it is hardly solid, even in its primary colors. There are major—perhaps irreparable—flaws in its construction.

Women

Jackson seems stronger on feminist issues and feminism itself than any candidate in history. From the start, he has said that political tickets must be "balanced" sexually and racially, not simply regionally or ideologically (that is, on the liberal-conservative spectrum). He has virtually promised to pick a woman as his running mate, and his insistence on political parity for women puts pressure on other Democrats to follow suit. Prominent black women are among his advisers. Shirley Chisholm, for example, was beside him when he announced his candidacy. But many feminists do not trust Jackson. They dislike his black Baptist style, they don't accept the macho attitudes of the black society he inhabits and they detect politically incorrect nuances in his public statements. For instance, when he invoked the names of Indira Gandhi, Golda Meir and Margaret Thatcher as proof that women can run governments, at the November 12 rally in Washington, D.C., against U.S. interventionist policies, many women in the throng booed. He must get a better sense of what his female audiences expect lest he alienate them irrevocably.

Blacks

The press picked up on black leaders' opposition to Jackson as soon as he started running. In a *60 Minutes* interview on the Sunday before Jackson announced, Mike Wallace ticked off what he thought was a damning litany of black critics: Coretta Scott King, Julian Bond, Andrew Young, Tom Bradley, Wilson Goode. It's a long list, although Jackson's roster of prominent black supporters is longer. But there are fundamental political differences between the two groupings. Many of Jackson's critics owe their status and power to white liberals and the Democratic Party. Some of them, King and Bond for example, have national white constituencies; the big-city Mayors in the group owe their elections to the white "swing" vote—whether it is 10 percent or 40 percent of the electorate. But leaders with a powerful black base (Congressional representatives from districts with black majorities, for instance) tend to be Jacksonians. And black voters seem far ahead of those critical leaders in their support for Jackson.

Jews

Jackson generally includes Jews among the rejected minorities he hopes to organize. In his announcement speech he said, "I know the pain of anti-Semitism because I have felt the humiliation of discrimination." His staff believes he will get substantial support from Jews on the left, some Jewish liberals and many Jewish students. But the tensions and antipathies that have developed between Jews and blacks in the last fifteen years cannot be overcome in a brief campaign. In many ways, Jews have led the opposition to black power in recent times. At least, their opposition has drawn attention in the media. Whereas major Jewish organizations supported the 1963 March on Washington, only a handful of Jewish groups joined in the twentieth anniversary demonstration. The reasons are familiar and well reported: black sympathy for the Palestinians, Jewish distaste for affirmative action quotas, and racism in both camps. Two weeks ago, an otherwise unidentified organization calling itself Jews Against Jackson signed a somewhat hysterical advertisement in *The New York Times.* Under a photograph of Jesse Jackson and Yasir Arafat in close embrace, the ad made it clear that Jackson was *very* bad for the Jews. The next day, Jewish leaders condemned the ad and the organization, which they said was a Jewish Defense League front. But hostility toward Jackson is widespread in the Jewish community, and there seems to be no way on earth for him to get significant contributions from those Jews who have traditionally filled liberal Democratic war chests.

The Left

If any group is excluded and ignored in American politics, it is the left. Leftists belong in the rainbow coalition, if anyone does, but many of them harbor strong objections to Jackson. For some, it is a matter of taste and style. Jackson and his people don't speak the left's language: they don't read the key books and magazines, go to the important political events, know the right movies, restaurants and resorts. Black funk is maddeningly different from left funk. Old and New Leftists have been proposing coalitions much like Jackson's for years, but the blacks were always supposed to join them, not lead them. Hard-line leftists worry that Jackson is not a Marxist ("He's like Maurice Bishop," one demonstrator at the November 12 rally told me. "He's more black than socialist"). Soft-line leftists worry about a white backlash to the campaign. John Judis, writing in *In These Times,* repeats Republican strategist Kevin Phillips's contention that Jackson will provoke white Southerners to come out in droves for Reagan, thus assuring the President's re-election.

Liberals

Jackson's coalition redefines political constituencies in America; it does not regard liberals and conservatives, for instance, or Northerners and Southerners, as having the kind of self-consciousness or class interests that would impel them to join an opposition movement. But liberals who sympathize with Jackson's campaign could make a big difference—*the* difference—in how well it succeeds. Liberal support, however, is far from assured. Liberals feel much more comfortable with ideas than with power, and Jackson, as Stoney Cooks said, "is about power." Jackson has not spelled out his position on many issues. What does he think about reindustrialization? Regulatory policy? The international debt crisis? In fact, the Jackson campaign seems to project an aura of power rather than to distribute an endless stream of position papers, and this image is unsettling to voters who choose their candidates on the basis of a careful weighing of "the issues." Such people might prefer George McGovern or Alan Cranston, who play their liberal politics the old-fashioned way. Neither of those candidates can now claim (as McGovern did in 1972) to be part of a powerful social or political movement, to be building political institutions beyond their candidacies, to have consequences beyond their likely defeat. The strength of Jackson's coalition is that it has the potential to loom larger, and to last longer, than the campaign that launches it.

The Poor

The rainbow coalition is a class action: it embraces those who do not have wealth and power and it opposes those who do. Although the coalition has corporate friends, it makes clear that the ruling class is the enemy. But the poor and the "welfare class"—or, more to the point, their organizers and spokespeople— may not see things that way. Jackson has never been keen on the welfare system; he says it creates dependence on government and is humiliating and debilitating. That is an opinion shared by the Republican right and the radical left, although those two groups propose diametrically opposite solutions to the "welfare mess." The right wants to dismantle the system; the left would substantially redistribute income and wealth. But some welfare organizers think Jackson will simply fuel the opposition to welfare without assembling the power to change it for the better. Writer-activists Frances Fox Piven and Richard Cloward have also been organizing a campaign to register low-paid workers and welfare recipients. They argue—in the same vein as Jackson—that those who do not vote make the crucial difference in elections, and that most nonvoters are from the excluded classes. The Piven-Cloward strategy, however, does not propose a candidate or campaign; it presumably would help any contender who promises quantitative and qualitative improvements in the social service system and other egalitarian economic measures. Jackson may get some benefits from that voter registration drive, but he will have to be clearer and firmer about his plans for change.

Beyond the problems of the rainbow coalition is the broader question of the future of the movement Jackson leads. The political mathematicians may figure out a theoretical way to beat the incredible odds and get him the nomination; but the only realistic forecast at this point shows Jackson going to the Democratic convention in San Francisco with a respectable but uncommanding block of votes; a wave of black support, some rainbow shine and an impressive record as a voter registration whiz. He might be able to parlay all that into the crucial margin of delegate support for one or another candidate. But the nomination could already be decided in the primaries. Does Jackson then bid for a Vice

Presidential nomination—for himself or, say, a woman he supports? Does he settle for a moment onstage with the white nominee, their hands clasped and their arms held high?

Does he walk out—or slip away—and begin the long, arduous and highly problematic effort of building an independent political movement, a permanent coalition of the people on the outside, the natural successor to the civil rights movement in its last days before Martin Luther King Jr. was killed? King had begun to broaden his constituency. He was adding "class" to "race" and "civil rights"; he was in Memphis in April 1968 to lead a garbage workers' strike. Jackson may have been boasting when he called himself King's successor, but he has the opportunity to make good on that claim now.

"I plan to have the longest and widest coattails of any candidate in this race," Jackson says, and he promises to field 10,000 rainbow candidates for office at every level in the 1984 election. That popular effort could be the foundation for a permanent movement outside the Democratic Party, with its own social institutions and political functions. "We don't need the Democrats or the Republicans," Jackson boasts, and he will try to prove his point. Opposition in America lacks a sustaining culture; Jackson's coalition offers the intriguing possibility of creating one.

The thrust of the campaign and the movement this fall may be discernible, but there is no way to see with any certainty what its shape will be next summer. The meaning has not yet "meaned" itself. Jesse Jackson is not the kind of public personality who has a master plan mapped out for years to come—as Kennedy was supposed to have had when he began his Presidential career in one Congressional district of Massachusetts. The movement is moving as fast under Jackson's feet as he can run with it, and there is no end to that course in sight.

EDITOR'S INTRODUCTION

The term 'Hispanics' denotes the Spanish-speaking people living throughout the United States, who presently number 14.6 million, or 6.4 per cent of the total population, according to the 1980 census. This extremely diverse group comprises Mexican-Americans, who live chiefly in the Southwest; Puerto Ricans (in the industrial Northeast as well as in Puerto Rico); Cubans (Florida); and people from sixteen other South and Central American countries who are United States residents. Whereas the total population of the United States increased about 50 per cent between 1950 and 1980, the Hispanic population increased by 270 per cent. If this trend continues the Hispanic population will number 47 million, or 15 per cent of the population, by the year 2020, so becoming the largest American minority group.

The relative youth of the Hispanic population, whose median age is 23, is perhaps even more significant than its sheer size. Because so many Hispanics have their whole lives—schooling, employment, and raising families—ahead of them, as a group they are certain to play an increasingly important role in American society. Although Hispanic political activism has been steadily evolving into a national force since the 1960s, Hispanics have not so far gained political influence or representation in proportion to their numbers. By 1984 there were eleven Hispanic congressmen, and one state governor. The reasons for this state of affairs, and the imminent prospect of a change in the political fortunes of Hispanic Americans, are described in this section.

First Thomas B. Morgan, writing in *Esquire,* asks whether the United States is becoming "latinized" or whether Spanish-speaking people are becoming Americanized. The second, third and fourth articles, from *National Journal, Miami Herald,* and *Washington Post,* describe politicians' efforts to woo the Hispanic voter in the 1984 Presidential election campaign, and the growing

sense that concerted action by the Hispanic community is long
overdue.

THE LATINIZATION OF AMERICA[1]

Thinking of oneself as an Anglo is hard for a liberal like me.
Anglo means "white, non-Hispanic," in the lingo of the nearly 15
million of my countrymen who have Hispanic (Spanish or Latin
American) roots—a number to which may be added 3 million
Puerto Ricans in Puerto Rico (U.S. citizens all, by act of Congress, 1917) and as many as 5 million Hispanic aliens residing
here now, mostly in the Southwest. *Anglo* is one of those words
that radiate meanings—from straight otherness to pejorative hostility. It grates on me, although not as much as *gringo* or *gabacho*.
I have always thought of myself as an American. I hold the view
that we really are one people, no matter how diverse. But hard
as it is to accept, I am an Anglo, too—a distinction that came to
me only last summer when the latinization of America suddenly
became a problem for me. Since then, I've been trying to work it
out.

It was a sunny day late in June, and crowds of people were
milling about on the streets of New York, where I live. There was
nothing special going on, no fiesta, no protest, no ethnic promotion. The car cards on my subway train, advertising everything
from Eastern Airlines to Preparation-H in Spanish, may have
started me thinking. I don't know. But walking up Fifth Avenue
toward my dentist's office, I felt concern (okay, fear)—abruptly,
it seemed—as I noticed I was hearing Spanish voices everywhere
and realized that I had been hearing them in shops, hotels, and
restaurants all over the city. It was as though New York had
achieved a kind of Hispanic critical mass. Nothing in particular
jarred me. I just noticed, felt surrounded by strangers and, for an
anxious moment, like Rip Van Winkle in my own home town.

[1]Reprint of an article by Thomas B. Morgan, a frequent contributor to *Esquire*. *Esquire*. 99:47–56.
My. '83. First published in *Esquire* magazine. Copyright © Thomas B. Morgan (1983).

The voices clicked together in my memory with scraps of information from here and there to form a picture of change, change of major proportions in my American life. And I began to worry. I suppose people have always worried me when I don't truly know who they are or what they are up to. Any change at all, in fact, troubles me when I don't understand it. I wanted to figure out exactly what was upsetting me.

Later, at home, as the picture emerged it looked something like this: In the papers and on the television news, Hispanic-angled stories had been appearing almost daily—"Hispanics Fastest-Growing U.S. Minority," "Hispanics Highest Birth Rate in U.S.," "Hispanics Expected to Outnumber Blacks Soon." One columnist estimated that the number of Hispanics had multiplied nearly ten times since 1940 while in the same period the nation's whole population did not even double. Talk about change! Then there was the Cuban-American story out of Miami—how they had arrived as political refugees after Castro's revolution, transformed that fatigued tourist and retirement city into a booming, bilingual, multinational business center, and then set about finding homes, cars, and jobs for another 100,000 refugees who had sailed in from Mariel on the Freedom Flotilla at Castro's whim. Perhaps most striking were those relentlessly regular stories about the troubled entries into this immigrant nation of more and more Hispanics from Puerto Rico as well as from Mexico, El Salvador, Guatemala, the Dominican Republic, Honduras, and almost all of the other nations of the Caribbean basin and South America. One expert predicted that a net increase of 500,000 Hispanic newcomers might be expected every year for the rest of this century. And when asked for comment, American spokesmen for the Hispanic community emphasized a consistent theme—the determination of their people as free Americans to maintain their Hispanic identity as they struggle to be included within the system.

I remember my first response. This picture, as far as it went, did not show a bad thing. The latinization of America could be seen as another chapter in our most enduring serial, the Americanization of everybody. In the first place, Hispanic fertility and immigration were only adding more energetic human beings to an ethnic community that had long since demonstrated its zeal for hard work, family virtues, and patriotism. Second, the Cubans in Miami were to be applauded, for, as *The Economist* would say, "Greater Miami is a city with a future in a western world full of cities with only a past." And third, preservation of group identity through language, food, music, religion, and custom had long been the fashion in the United States, which prides itself on being the most successful multiethnic society in the world.

But there was more to the picture, and the source of my alarm turned up there, among stories I'd heard and read about the resistance of middle-class Hispanics to the difficult but (I think) necessary process of assimilation. Since the Seventies there had been a highly publicized Hispanic drive for bilingualism: Spanish-language courses for the transitional training of school kids, as well as maintenance programs for further education in Spanish, with English perhaps as a second language; ballots in Spanish for Hispanic voters as a permanent requirement of election law; even road signs in Spanish for Hispanic motorists. What might come next? The *Congressional Record* in Spanish as well as English? The State of the Union Message with Spanish subtitles? Or, further out, a Quebec-style solution to the problems of integration? That's where I got alarmed: I could imagine a scenario for the latinization of America leading to a divided nation—two Americas, one speaking English, one speaking Spanish.

Farfetched? Not really. Not with a critical mass of Spanish-speaking voters settling in city after city of the nation. Not when Hispanics, too, were expressing concern about the antiassimilationist trend among them. Last spring, for example, a California-born Mexican-American writer, Richard Rodriguez, had sent me a copy of his new book, *Hunger of Memory*. One passage read: "Today I hear bilingual educators say that children lose a degree of 'individuality' by becoming assimilated into public society. . . . But the bilingualists simplistically scorn the value and necessity of assimilation. . . . Dangerously, middle-class ethnics romanticize public separateness and trivialize the dilemma of the socially disadvantaged."

Played out, I realized, the separatist scenario could put an end to my liberal dream of one people and a so-called Americanist future. Then came the hard part: self-recognition. I had to admit that, after all, the choice of a Hispanic future finally rested with the Hispanics. And I had to acknowledge that my alarm, frankly, was that of not only a liberal but an Anglo who did not want to pay for the maintenance of *their* language, did not want to have to learn Spanish in order to get around in his own country, and did not even want to contemplate the turmoil that was sure to arise if America opted for a dual future. That is what I mean by self-recognition. As I say, it was hard, but it also prompted me to find out what I could about the Hispanic future, to talk about that future with Hispanic leaders around the country, to remind myself of what I already knew. And when I remembered the individual Mexican-Americans and Puerto Ricans I had met in my life, I wondered that the shock of self-recognition had been so long in coming.

The first and best Hispanic friend I ever had was a Mexican-American steam fitter named Jesse Saldana. In the summer of 1944 we worked together at a shipyard in Wilmington, California, where Victory ships were built. I was Jesse's assistant. He taught me all that I needed to know about plumbing, and he liked to hear me talk about my home town—Springfield, Illinois—because it was Abraham Lincoln's home town, too. I confessed to him that I had never met a Mexicano before. A Greek family ran the "Mexican" chilli (two *l*'s) parlor in Springfield, and, as far as I knew, they never had a Mexicano customer. Jesse knew a lot of Mexican history, about which I had learned little in school. It was he who told me that the United States Army had occupied Mexico City in 1847, enabling President Polk to persuade the Mexican government to take $15 million for the northern third of its real estate—California, Arizona, New Mexico, Utah, and Nevada. Fifty years later, Jesse also taught me, a similarly persuasive occupation gained us Puerto Rico. Jesse admitted to me that he was virtually illiterate, that he had a serious police record, and that he was wanted by the sheriff of Reno, Nevada. Still, he used to say, he thought he could have done better in his time if it had not been for Anglo prejudice against Mexicanos. He was particularly angry, he said, about the mass deportations of Mexicanos during the Thirties and about the way the Los Angeles police behaved during the "Zoot Suit Riots" of 1943. In bloody

detail, he described the street battles he said he had seen between
Mexicano youths and Anglo servicemen. His wrath peaked, as I
recall, just as he told how the local cops consistently moved in on
the side of the soldiers and sailors. "Justice is blind," Jesse often
said. "She can't see the Mexicans." In the fall, after I had returned
home to get ready for the Army, Jesse sent me a newspaper clip-
ping describing another such "riot." I wrote back, saying I was on
his side, but I never heard from him again. His anger, though,
would be unforgettable.

In the early Sixties I befriended another Mexican-American:
Mayor Juan Cornejo of Crystal City, Texas. His town of 9,500
people in the dusty southwestern part of the state called itself the
"Spinach Capital of the World." It had long discouraged reckless
Hispanic participation in the democratic process until it elected
Cornejo, thirty-three, a business agent for the Teamsters union at
the spinach packinghouse. The election shocked all of Texas. It
became an instant legend, and a New York magazine editor sent
me to Crystal City to write a story about it. Local people were
talking about threats of reprisals against Cornejo's supporters,
and some thought that the mayor himself might be in danger. In
fact, Cornejo survived both his term and the national publicity.
But I would remember his concern that I might get hurt for coming to Crystal City to write about the Anglos' comeuppance. And
I never forgot his feistiness, which had inspired the subtitle for the
story I wrote: "The Texas Giant Awakens."

Around Cornejo's time, there were other Mexicano stirrings.
"Viva Kennedy" clubs, set up for the Presidential campaign of
1960, brought a new generation of Mexicanos into mainstream
politics all over the Southwest. Aside from the *patron* system in
Democratic New Mexico, neither party in the region had both-
ered with that sort of thing before, at least partly because the
Mexicano vote had not been large enough to matter. Mexicanos
organized opposition to the Federal *bracero* program (whereby
farm workers were imported under contract) and helped kill it.
Cesar Chavez began his nonviolent fight for recognition of a farm
workers' union by California growers. And young Mexicanos
chose the name Chicano to express ethnic pride; they called for
"brown power" and were echoed by young Puerto Ricans in New

York. Looking back with the clarity of hindsight, I saw that the awakening of those days was oversold. The Sixties did not exactly ring in a new era for Hispanics—indeed, the concept of Hispanics as a kind of superethnic group did not exist at that time—but *something* did happen, more like an alarm clock going off three hours before dawn.

In the early Seventies, when I worked at City Hall in New York with Mayor John Lindsay, I got to know half a dozen Puerto Rican mayoral aides. It was significant then, I now realized, that hardly twenty years after the start of the great migration from the island to the city, New York's desperately underprivileged Puerto Rican community was beginning to claim some share of local patronage. I also got to know Herman Badillo, who in 1970 became the first Puerto Rican ever sent to Congress from New York and the first ever to vote in the House. Badillo's election gave mainland Puerto Ricans an impressive voice in Washington. Moreover, by visibly linking Puerto Ricans and Mexicanos (represented by congressmen from California, New Mexico, and Texas) at the national level, his presence in Washington seemed a step in the direction of creating a national Hispanic identity, and future.

But the truth remains, before last summer's apotheosis the latinization of America was rarely on my mind. And when it was, the context was most likely to be an impersonal occasion—a press conference on the housing crisis in the Bronx, a street festival, a Puerto Rican Day parade, a fund-raiser for Cesar Chavez, an FALN bombing, or Cuban roast pig at Victor's Café in Manhattan. Hispanics as real people were neither my daily reality nor my foremost liberal concern—*that* was the problem of race and poverty among black Americans. As a reporter, I had interviewed Martin Luther King Jr. many times—first, during the Montgomery bus strike, and last, in Chicago, where he was making his stand for the integration of the North. His last movement had failed, utterly. And there had followed—in direct response, I thought—the victory of the "new ethnicity" on the playing fields of American ideologies. I had never celebrated that victory. I put it down as yet another part of the Hispanic picture that was worrying me.

Maybe it was my age. I had grown up in the Thirties and For-
ties with the ideology of integration through assimilation, the
American melting pot, and a hoped-for common civilization to
which all could belong and to which all could contribute, eventually achieving no less than a "composite American identity," as Walt
Whitman had promised. Just thinking about it last summer made
me gasp at how uncool Americanism had become. Yet, *e pluribus
unum,* onenationindivisible, equality-in-freedom, and the picture
of everyone praying together on Norman Rockwell's Four Freedoms poster—that was us.

America was something else, too. It was a deal—first Square,
then New, then Fair. Each immigrant's son and the son of each
immigrant's son (I am one of those, grandson of Polish and Roma-
nian Jewish immigrants) knew in his bones the terms of *his* deal.
You traded memory for opportunity, the Old Country for the New
World, culture for power, identity for rights. And if, after you became Americanized, you cared to retrieve the past, argue about
dual commitments, biculturism, and ethnic survival, and teach
your children a language you yourself may have denied, you were
welcome. But making the deal and becoming included was the first
order of business. Funny, you still felt your own ethnic self, and
all the more an American because it was a seamless relationship;
you really felt as though you belonged to an American peoplehood.
And despite all the nativist, racist loons who had tried to take
charge of this Americanist ideal, our peoplehood was what we believed we were defending in World War II. It made possible whatever else we wanted to be or do, ethnically or otherwise. Sit in
wonder, generations. Think what you will. But this was how we
were and what we believed.

At some point in the Sixties, though—it may have been just
before or just after Stokely Carmichael raised his fist and told
whitey to get lost—some people I knew began quoting a book
(quoting the title, at least) by Nathan Glazer and Daniel Patrick
Moynihan, *Beyond the Melting Pot,* and telling one another that
the ingredients in the melting pot hadn't really melted; that ours
had been a pluralistic society all along; that we needed a "new
ethnicity" to maintain stability in our polyglot cities (then aflame);
and that facing our diversity was better and easier than facing the

failure of black integration in the North. Dead were Medgar Evers, Martin Luther King Jr., and Robert Kennedy. Dead or dying was integration through assimilation. The goal of democracy was not to be equality for individuals after all but, rather, making the world safe for diversity among groups. And with amazing speed, that America of the new ethnicity materialized with more pluralistic fissures than a Tiffany lamp.

It was easy then, as regards the problem of race, to prescribe for black "rhetoric" a new American policy of benign neglect. Furthermore, as political scientist Michael Mandelbaum had told me, the passion for ethnicity meant to some people that you didn't have to assimilate to make it in America. And when the word *Hispanic* emerged (the U.S. Census used it for the first time on its 1980 forms), it would be hailed as a direct expression of the new American ideology. As Congressman Robert Garcia, successor to Herman Badillo, would exclaim to me: "Six years ago, you didn't see the word *Hispanic*. Now it's a word that everyone can coalesce under. This is the news!"

The stage was set for the Eighties—"the decade of the Hispanics," someone had called it. The picture was complete. And here was the nub of my fear about the Hispanic future. A prolonged process (twenty years? fifty years?) of Americanization is under way. But we are going into it under a new dispensation, as ethnics all, Hispanics and Anglos (and black, Asians, and Native Americans). We have no Americanist ideal to see us through, no sense of the nation more lofty than our private identities. Only the challenge is not new: to acculturate and integrate over time yet another great immigrant people.

Census reports and other data I collected helped define the nature of that challenge.

First, they showed the sheer variety of the latinizers of America. Hispanics come from thirty Latin American countries, plus Spain and Portugal. Ethnically and historically, Mexicans, Puerto Ricans, and Cubans (the three largest Hispanic groups in the U.S.) differ from one another as much as the Irish, the English, and the Scotch do. The rest have their differences, too. Each group has its own national memories and its own racial characteristics. Broadly, *Hispanic* may be taken to mean Latin American brown, like European white, African black, and Asian yellow. But such connotations only make life simpler for demographers. Hispanics are actually white, black, or Indian, or a mix of two or of all three. *Hispanic* also may mean "of Spanish-speaking origin or descent," but the first language of Hispanics from Latin America may be Portuguese, French, or even English. And in America, immigrant Hispanics tend to use English when necessary and speak Spanish at home; the vast majority of American-born Hispanics are bilingual. Religious preference further complicates the meaning of *Hispanic*. Although there is a Catholic majority, church attendance is far below that of non-Hispanic Catholics. And significant numbers are Protestants, born-agains, Jews, Baptists, and Mormons. Some, of course, don't believe.

Second, the facts disabused me of the vague ideas I had about where Hispanics live. It was news to me that twenty-five cities in the nation now have Hispanic communities of 50,000 or more— from the largest, Los Angeles (2 million, mostly Mexican, some Salvadoran), to Chicago (422,000, mainly Mexican and Puerto Rican), Denver (92,000, mostly Mexican), and Philadelphia (63,000, mostly Puerto Rican). Over half the 1.46 million Hispanics in New York are Puerto Rican, but some of these may be among an estimated 400,000 Dominican aliens in the city, some of whom call themselves Puerto Ricans in order to become instantly naturalized. And even in cities where the Hispanic population is less than 50,000, their number is significant as a percentage of the whole. In Hartford, Connecticut, for example, 20 percent of the population of 136,000 is Hispanic. It turns out that Hispanics are not rural people. About 85 percent reside in metropolitan areas. It may be politically significant someday that they have tended to settle in influential states—4.5 million in California (19 percent of the superstate), nearly 3 million in powerful Texas, and 1.7 million in media-rich New York. But there is also a notable trend toward dispersal. After decades of concentration, the census data showed, Hispanics are moving to cities in all parts of the country, taking their future with them.

Third, unofficial projections that I studied indicated a potentially dramatic rise in the Hispanic population as a percentage of the whole population over the next generation. The 1980 census counted 14.6 million Hispanics in the United States. Estimates of undocumented Hispanics ranged from 1 million to 10 million, with most in the middle range; the 5-million guess I have made may be too high or too low by 2 million. Now, assuming 20 million Hispanic citizens and aliens in America, a continuation of present high birth rates (although these could change with increasing prosperity), and continued immigration at, say, 500,000 annually (this could change, too, under a new immigration law), Hispanics would number 35 million in a nation of 280 million *seventeen years* from now. And if that were the combination, Hispanics in the year 2000 would be not only the largest American "minority" group, ahead of blacks by a small margin, but also the largest of all groups—ahead of WASPs (now leading, with 29 million) and Germans (second today, with more than 25 million). It's true that then there would be 200 million Anglos, over 33 million blacks, and about 10 million Asians. Still, the Hispanic share of the population would rise to more than 12 percent by the millennium. And the meaning of that seemed clear: Hispanics could be a unique force for change in the country by then, depending upon the way the challenge of their future had been met.

My summer's journey in search of Hispanic America took me from New York to Washington, the Southwest, and Florida. Some sixty-odd Hispanic leaders gave me their observations on the future. Traveling around with my liberal biases in tow, I gained some insight into where, after all, the latinization of America may be taking us. I even learned a little about how to play my new role as an Anglo for as long as it may be required. In the end, I emerged with a new picture of Hispanic America in my mind.

Early on, I decided to look up Victor Marrero, one of the Puerto Rican aides to Mayor Lindsay. Marrero had since served as chairman of the New York City Planning Commission and as Undersecretary of Housing and Urban Development in the Carter administration. He now practices law in Manhattan. From his success story I took away an awful sense of the waste of others like him who had been unable to escape the barrio. Marrero was born in the slums of San Juan in 1941. He moved with his family to New York in 1951 and entered the fourth grade, speaking only Spanish. In 1964 he graduated from New York University; in

1968, from Yale Law School. Today, at forty-one, he is a slim, soft-spoken man with a long, square face and thinning hair. He offered to take me to the South Bronx for lunch at Mama Aponte's restaurant on Southern Boulevard, not far from where he used to live. On the way, we drove through block after block of abandoned apartment buildings, some tilted crazily to one side but still standing because the city has no money for demolition. We passed the vast emptiness of the Charlotte Street site that President Carter had visited in 1977, promising a rebirth of the area that was later stillborn. *The Wall Street Journal* had said that week that better times were coming to the South Bronx, that new developments were coming off the drafting tables, but Marrero was skeptical. In one recent five-year period, he told me, while five hundred units of housing were being built in the Bronx, *fifty thousand* units were lost through decay, abandonment, and arson.

"When I got here as a kid," Marrero said, "it was the pits. But there were people in the school system willing to make things happen for me. There was no one to advise me, except the school. My teacher encouraged me to take the exam to go to the Bronx High School of Science, and I was picked. In my class of seven hundred fifty, there were maybe ten blacks and one or two Puerto Ricans. I went there full of apprehension, but I finished that first year seventh in my class."

Marrero's experience is not unique, but it is far from that of most of the Puerto Ricans who, as conditions worsened on the island in the Fifties, had flocked to New York looking for work.

"We were classic immigrants," Marrero said. "We thought the streets were paved with gold. The typical Puerto Rican was a jibaro—a hillbilly—from the mountains or the rural areas. It was, you might say, a mass migration of hillbillies from Kentucky, plus no English. The average Puerto Rican came with no skills, no education. He was not even literate in Spanish."

The surprise was that the country was not expanding as it had been when earlier waves of immigrants had landed. Good jobs required a high school education or better. During the Sixties and Seventies, New York was losing 500,000 manufacturing jobs, becoming a service-economy town. Now, little remains for unskilled workers other than bottom-rung jobs in restaurants, stores, and hotels.

"Many of us cannot survive here," Marrero said, "so we go back and forth quickly. There is a feeling of being a transient, of being temporary. You yearn for your own farm back on the island. You lack incentive to get involved in the community. Meanwhile, you hear more and more about democratic pluralism, which means America is no longer intended to be a whole country, but a system for monitoring the parts. We were never a part of the mainstream, and now this. So you see, for the future, it's a special problem."

After lunch, Marrero showed me a housing project he had shepherded through to completion during his term in Washington. It is home to Puerto Ricans and to blacks, who share, along with all Hispanics, double billing in the long-running American tragedy of race. Yet, perhaps for the saddest of reasons—skin color—Puerto Ricans are making relatively quicker progress than blacks. Unemployment through the recession, for example, has been lower among Hispanics than among blacks, though higher than among Anglos. Accordingly, efforts to coordinate the political activities of blacks and Hispanics are having less than middling success. Competition for jobs, especially minority political appointments, has created conflict as Hispanic clout rises and opportunities decline. Job-seeking Hispanic aliens have further divided the two groups. Yet, despite these tensions, Marrero believes Puerto Ricans may be destined to be a key to what he calls "America's most delicate problem": the problem of race.

"Puerto Ricans," he said, "do not have the sense of discrimination toward skin colors that other people do. There are many mixed marriages. We have a society on the island that has overcome the trauma of race. You can see it here in the city. Puerto Ricans live next door to blacks. They coexist without the kind of explosion that has occurred when there is an Irish-black or an Italian-black situation. This is the positive contribution we can make to America."

That the Puerto Ricans, given their own tenuous situation, should be the Americans to make that contribution struck me as ironic indeed.

After poverty and race, the other undeniable problem most Hispanics face is continuing Hispanic immigration. Although achievement by second- and third-generation Hispanics is beginning to resemble traditional immigrant patterns, the relentless pressure of new immigrants on limited resources can't help but check the progress of the community as a whole. Immigration, however, is not something the Hispanic community can control. It is essentially a function of both U.S. laws and the poverty or politics of the Latin American nations. A cooperative hemispheric attack on mass poverty in Mexico and the Caribbean basin might hold back the tide, but no one I talked to in Washington expected that to happen. A more effective U.S. immigration law could help. Last summer Congress was struggling to bring to a vote the Simpson-Mazzoli bill, by which Hispanics (both citizens and aliens) had the most to gain or to lose. Proposed sanctions against employers of alien workers raised fears of discrimination against anyone who looked "alien"—that is, Hispanic; but the bill also proposed amnesty for many illegal aliens now in residence. The real case for Simpson-Mazzoli was simply that it had a chance of passing both Houses in a country desperately divided over immigration reform. It failed.

The crisis of enforcing existing laws continues. The cost of guarding our coasts and two thousand miles of borderline between Mexico and the United States is all but prohibitive. New ways to beat the Immigration and Naturalization Service crop up all the time. The latest passage is through Canada: aliens fly in from the Caribbean basin and have themselves driven across the border by an American relative or a hired Anglo driver. The U.S. has yet to devise an effective monitoring system for temporary but legal alien workers, many of whom simply work out their allotted time and stay on as illegals. Most, it appears, continue to work, and many pay taxes; yet the fear of deportation limits their freedom and, I was told, isolates them. Though it is unmeasurable, the impetus that 5 million Hispanic illegals give to separatism must be considerable.

After a time, I began to understand that the link between poverty, race, and immigration, so far as the Hispanics were concerned, is first and foremost the issue of economic opportunity. For the citizen majority as well as the legal and illegal alien minority, a chance to make good is *the* priority. I wanted to discuss economic opportunity with Cesar Chavez, who had invited me to visit him in Salinas, California, during a break in negotiations with the local lettuce growers.

Salinas is a pink- and orange-brick town that cannot seem to make up its mind whether its heart belongs to John Steinbeck or John Wayne. Chavez, too, seemed a man with his heart in two places: he is an activist doing the job of a manager. There is a human and a technological limit to the further growth of his union. Once the very image of the Mexicano, the field workers have greatly declined in number, along with all agricultural employees. The peonage system that dominated the life of the Mexicano was destroyed by Chavez and the union. But gains in wages and working conditions hastened the mechanization of the farm business. The result: Better jobs, but fewer of them, and an aging union. For Chavez, it has meant carrying on quietly with no new worlds to conquer. Nowadays, he told me, he is concentrating on the union's internal structure and on doing a better job for the men and women still in the fields, using computers to keep their records straight and the latest communication techniques to keep them informed. He was also facing a bitter intraunion challenge from dissident members that had embarrassed him. Chavez, fifty-six, is a vegetarian, short and stocky, with small hands.

"The issues for Hispanics," he said, "are the same as for everyone else now: unemployment, high interest rates, crime. Our differences are over opportunities. But even there we have come a long way from the Thirties. It is a different world. Even the same bridges I slept under don't look the same anymore, though I guess they would if I had to sleep under them again. You see, time is the element. We Hispanics are, finally, like other immigrant groups."

I asked him whether Hispanics are moving forward fast enough and far enough to satisfy him.

"No," he said, "change is not happening to everyone, not yet. But the barriers are not insurmountable. When I was a kid, our identity was strong within our own group. We hid our tacos and our tortillas. Today we promote them. Today identity means getting more professionals into good jobs. It means getting more influence so others can get breaks. Yes, the Hispanics are going to become more like the majority. Their families will be smaller, better educated, more traveled. Roots will be lost. Language will be lost. Food will be the last to go. We will be eating tacos and tortillas for a long time to come."

Later in the summer I received a similar message back in New York from a Puerto Rican businessman named John Torres, who sells mountains of groceries wholesale. His customers are the proprietors of bodegas, the mom-and-pop neighborhood grocery stores that are often the beginning of economic independence for thousands of ambitious Hispanic couples. In New York alone, Torres told me, there are 6,500 bodegas. He is a small, fiftyish, wiry man with great energy.

"Do you know what this country is all about?" he asked me. "It is all about running a business. You won't have people on welfare if they see something—an opportunity. Isn't that what this is, a land of opportunity? I want to help my country! I want to make our people independent. I don't want them crying poverty anymore. I want them to say, 'Don't give me a fish. Show me how to fish.'"

The statement stuck in my mind for two reasons. One was the emphasis on opportunity. The other was the style. As Torres talked to me I was reminded of nothing so much as long-ago days listening to my father, a second-generation small-businessman in furniture, declaiming on the very same values.

America, however, is not only about running a business but also about running a country. It follows that political opportunity will profoundly influence Hispanics' choice of futures. And, as I found out, that political opportunity was being tested at that very moment—one way in San Antonio, another way in Miami.

Given their numbers, Hispanics can be expected to bring forward new leaders and do better in U.S. politics than they have done so far. But this is not to say that they have not seen some opportunities already. Ten years ago, there were five Hispanics in the U.S. House of Representatives and one in the Senate. A year ago there were six in the House, none in the Senate. As I write there are nine in the House—one Puerto Rican (Robert Garcia of New York) and eight Mexicanos (Manuel Lujan Jr., the lone Republican, and Bill Richardson of New Mexico; Henry Gonzalez, E "Kika" de la Garza, and Solomon Ortiz of Texas; and Edward Roybal, Matthew Martinez, and Esteban Torres of California). The new governor of New Mexico is Toney Anaya, a Mexicano. The mayor of San Antonio, Henry Cisneros, is a Mexicano, and the mayor of Miami, Maurice Ferré, is a Puerto Rican. The number of Hispanics elected and appointed to positions at the mid-levels of state and local governments across the country is higher than ever before.

Still, the opportunities taken have not overwhelmed the usual political observers. The only Hispanic among the top jobholders in the Reagan administration is John Hernandez, who was hastily appointed acting administrator of the Environmental Protection Agency after the resignation of Anne McGill Burford in March. There are no Hispanics in the United States Senate, on the Los Angeles City Council, or on the Los Angeles County Board of Supervisors. Hispanic voters appear to have had only limited influence on the outcome of last fall's general election, too. In two of the three most "Hispanic" states, New York and California, Hispanic voter turnout did not come close to its potential; only one third of the eligible Hispanics in New York are registered. In Texas, though, Hispanic power seems real, and it may be that Texas is in the process of helping to create the next Hispanic leader with national charisma, the first since Cesar Chavez.

When I got to San Antonio, I found that this process depends largely on thirty-eight-year-old William Velasquez, an ebullient man who runs the Southwest Voter Registration Education Project out of a suite of vinyl offices in downtown San Antonio. Since 1975 the project has labored to raise the level of Hispanic and Native American political activity through 518 voter drives in 132 communities throughout the Southwest. One indication of success: Between the 1976 and 1980 Presidential elections, Mexicano registrations increased by 664,695 names and votes cast increased by 313,504. Velasquez told me how it happened:

"Always before," he said, "Mexicanos have been herded into the polls every four years to vote for President. This time we assembled lists of potential voters and polled them to find out what they wanted. The biggest issues were local ones—drainage and education. So we based our voter-registration drive on our polling results, not on the national issues. It was the greatest increase in registration and turnout in history."

I asked Velasquez how the Anglo community had reacted.

"It's important," he said, "to say that the Anglos in the Southwest are maturing, too. The Southwest is not as intransigent as it once was. We used to get threatening letters and phone calls. 'You'll be killed! Shot! Watch it!' But there's been none of that since 1976."

The outstanding beneficiary of changing times and the voter project is San Antonio's charismatic mayor, Henry Cisneros. Elected in 1981, Cisneros became the first Mexicano to capture City Hall. He had defeated an Anglo opponent when, for the first time in the city's history, the Mexicanos' voter turnout exceeded the Anglos'. He still teaches public administration at the local branch of the University of Texas (he keeps his job because the salary of the mayor of San Antonio is fifty dollars a week). At thirty-five, he lives in a small house in the neighborhood where he grew up on the modest but proud Hispanic West Side of San Antonio. Nearby is a housing project decorated with vibrant, primary-colored wall paintings commemorating highlights of *Mexicanidad*—Montezuma, Zapata, the Sixteenth of September (Mexican Independence Day), Archbishop Flores, and Medal of Honor winner Cleto Rodriguez. Cisneros looks like an El Greco figure—lean, dark, and hollow-cheeked. You sense that, given his life chance, he could go for broke (running statewide in Texas, for example) or—under different circumstances—retire from the field like a bullfighter who knows when his day is past. In his office one afternoon, with a bust of John F. Kennedy looking down from a bookcase, Cisneros acknowledged that while he was an important symbol to the Mexican-American community, he was also a politician who could be beaten. He had had to move to the right politically in order to work with the San Antonio business community.

"If I run for reelection," he said, "my opposition could be from the left, from a Hispanic candidate, while my support among the Anglos could be stronger."

As mayor, Cisneros had set himself the goal of encouraging both business and integration in San Antonio. He wanted San Antonio to be the first minority city to incorporate that minority into the mainstream. He was working toward it last summer. And he seemed to believe it could be done if Hispanics are able to take advantage of high-tech jobs that new industry has to offer.

"We are going now," he said, "into a society that draws a line between the technologically competent and the technologically incompetent. I think we will find that this line will be harder to cross than those of race, religion, or ethnicity." Then he looked further into the future. "I feel Hispanics themselves—the Mexicanos, the Puerto Ricans, the Cubans—will tend to merge," he said. "They are already assimilating among one another, thinking of themselves as Hispanics, in the Midwest. In turn, they will assimilate into the mainstream for economic progress. Here in cities like San Antonio, El Paso, Albuquerque, where the streams of immigrants constantly replenish the community, Hispanics will control more and more institutions—school boards, local government, businesses—and even become dominant. But everywhere they will be free-enterprise-oriented, loaded with American values but Hispanic-oriented as well."

Cisneros may be a star. His town seems to be on a roll: it has five new skyscrapers, and the newspapers are full of talk about new industries coming in. There is a dynamic in San Antonio that is working for him. But he is in the middle between entrenched Anglo forces opposed to change and activist Mexicanos who have no time to wait. If he succeeds, his style and substance could be an example for a generation of Hispanic leaders to follow.

Landing in Miami on a warm day last August, I realized I had not been there since the Democratic Convention of 1972, when my party nominated George McGovern for President, my man Lindsay having been defeated earlier in the political season, right there in the Florida primary. In those days, the Cuban-American community was more exiled than expansive. The mayor was an Anglo. So were the hands working all the levers of power. This time I was picked up at the airport by a Cuban businessman who drove me into town along the booster route—down palm-studded Brickell Avenue to see the glorious, brand-new hotels and apartments; off on a side street to gawk at a tree growing through a hole in a skyscraper; around dizzying curves and across a causeway over

Biscayne Bay to stare, on the other side, at a new, *fabuloso,* slant-sided high-rise; and then, in a wink, back through the bustling main drag—before he left me to check in at the Inter-Continental Hotel. Everyone said this was the place to gape at the mysterious rich from down south who have taken to calling Miami the capital of Latin America. Since it was hot summertime, I did not see any signs of real gold at the hotel, but there's no doubt that Miami has something going on in addition to its racial problems and its crime wave.

In daylight, Miami really hums. Still at night, it reminded me of the old days in New York when everyone, all at once, acquired his first television set and stayed home and off the streets every night for about four years. Miami's problem was not television; it was fear of crime. Even Cubans were telling me not to be walking around town after dark if I valued my safety, and Miami is *their* town.

I went to see Mayor Maurice Ferré at City Hall, which rests like a white whale in a huge parking lot partially surrounded by yachts in a gorgeous basin. Ferré is the scion of a renowned dynastic family of Ponce, Puerto Rico. He had been mayor since 1973, winning five times over both Anglo and Cuban challengers by putting together a coalition of all races, including blacks. He is a crisp, dapper man, said to be a deep student of the Cuban soul. He seemed to understand what I was thinking: that if Hispanic separatism was going anywhere, the Cubans would get there with it first. Ferré laid it all out for me.

"You have three Hispanic worlds," he said. "The Cubans are quite unlike the Mexicans and the Puerto Ricans. The Cubans, first of all, are an exile community, similar to the White Russians in Paris. They are not immigrants. Second, the Cubans are almost one hundred percent literate in Spanish. Third, the Cubans are educated. Most have high school degrees as a minimum. Fourth, racially, they are a whiter group, so they can assimilate, they can intermarry with less difficulty. And fifth, they have a common cause: the freedom of Cuba. They are different, because they can't go home again. They hate being called Hispanics."

I said to Ferré that Miami seemed to be a place where it was possible to live entirely in Spanish.

"So it is," he said. "You can be born here in a Cuban hospital, be baptized by a Cuban priest, buy all your food from a Cuban grocer, take your insurance from a Cuban broker, and pay for it all with a check from a Cuban bank. You can get all the news in Spanish—read the Spanish daily paper, watch Spanish TV, listen to Spanish radio. You can go through life without having to speak English at all."

To hear Ferré tell it, fifty years from now the Cubans will be both integrated and still speaking Spanish. But how could they assimilate without learning English?

In 1974 the Supreme Court ruled that school districts must take steps to ensure that students who lack English language skills are not denied an education. Many schools adopted transitional instruction in the students' native language. That policy seemed reasonable to me. But the future Ferré described would mean maintenance teaching of Spanish at all taxpayers' expense. "Why?" I asked.

"We demand this," Ferré said, "because we recognize that culture is vitally important if we are going to be able to solve our problems. The thing that rescues people is pride—pride in their religion, their family, their tradition, their language. As I see it, what is great about America is the system of the Constitution and citizenship. It works because citizenship is what makes us all Americans. Language is not necessary to the system. Nowhere does the Constitution say that English is our language. If you are a cynic, you will say that we will have a balkanized nation. If you are an optimist, you believe that the Hispanics will wind up like everyone else. They will have a little impact, add a little flavor, a few different values. But fifty years from now, the Hispanics will be like everyone else. Only Miami will be different."

I chewed on that most of the evening and while flying home the next morning. I had a vision of Miami not as Quebec but, rather, like a little Switzerland. In Switzerland many languages are spoken and all banks are silent. Close, but quite different. Miami is a city that is 40 percent non-Cuban. Do the Anglos and the blacks leave? Do they live as expatriates in their own town? Does Miami become a functioning, officially Spanish enclave in America? No doubt, Miami was doing well. But it could become a balkanized state. I guess that makes me a cynic.

Back in New York, mulling over my impressions of the Hispanics I had talked with around the country, it seemed to me that
the community's cultural life, like its leadership, inevitably reflected the dilemma within the community itself. Culture transfers
style, traditions, ideas through cultural products within the group
not only for the group's survival; it also enables the group to establish kinship with others. In an immigrant society like ours, cultural products have long marked the spot where assimilation and
ethnicity meet. I had observed that Hispanic and Anglo were
meeting there now. As never before, Hispanic cultural products
were in demand among Anglos—salsa music, tequila, and rum,
fast food at Chi-Chis, a good guy on *Hill Street Blues,* a bad guy
in the new movie *Scarface.* There is also an exploding interest not
only in the giants of Latin American literature but also in Hispanic writers of promise homegrown in the United States (Piri Thomas, Edward Rivera, John Rechy, Richard Rodriguez, Rudolfo
Anaya, Luis Valdez). As in politics, participation in the larger
culture eases the way toward integration.

Yet there is a separatist countertrend: the growth of cultural
products in Spanish for an ever-growing Hispanic market. In
1980 the projected income for all U.S. Hispanics was more than
$70 billion, making a market of $40 billion for consumer goods.
This gave an economic basis to the impetus toward bilingualism
as more and more marketers attempted to reach the Hispanic consumer through Spanish-language television, radio, and newspapers. The specialists in Hispanic marketing are, of course, mostly
Hispanics. In Miami I had met Teri Zubizarreta, a Cuban woman ("Call me Zubi") who runs her own advertising agency for the
Spanish market only. Zubi gave me an example of the nuances of
Hispanic advertising.

"There is a noticeable response," she said, "when an advertiser
takes the trouble to think our way. You cannot simply translate
English-language copy into Spanish and expect the same response. You take Pepsi-Cola. Their slogan was, Catch that Pepsi
spirit. If we had put that straightaway into Spanish, viewers
would have considered it voodoo, something about a spirit flying
through the air. So we changed it to read, *Vive el sentir de Pepsi.*
That means, Live that Pepsi feeling. That's what the English slo-

gan intends to say, but you have to know the idiosyncracies of the market to put it across."

In the end, the Hispanic future I had first pictured did not square with the reality I had found. Hispanic America is, in fact, moving along two paths, pushed by the new ethnicity but pulled by the need to assimilate. Rhetoric and headlines push. The knowledge of what it takes to survive in America pulls. From the new picture in my mind, I sensed which might prevail. I wanted to test it and turned to Richard Rodriguez, whose book, *Hunger of Memory,* had helped stir my Anglo angst. In his book Rodriguez described the pain of separation that occurs in a Spanish-speaking family as the children learn English in an American grade school, and having described it (as he lived it in California), he pronounced it profoundly necessary.

Rodriguez came by last fall in New York on his way from San Francisco, where he lives, to London, where he was going to lecture. At thirty-seven, he is a swarthy, intense man with a zone of somber remoteness behind the eyes. One hostile reviewer from San Antonio called him a "displaced person," and he seems displaced, but in the good sense, like Don Quixote, who found himself in the wrong century. I told him of the picture of Hispanic America that I had contrived over the summer. He replied:

"I think this is what's going on—that America is based on a consensus that we all forget the past, and then some Hispanics have come along to say that, hey, you've made a mistake. The irony, of course, is that Mexico itself is an assimilationist country. What is Mexico, if it is not Mayan, Spanish, Irish, Jewish? They all went there in the eighteenth century. They built Mexico on the medieval Catholic idea of one people in a single city.

"Today," Rodriguez went on, "you find some middle-class Mexican-Americans courting ethnicity. They are refusing to speak English to their children. But this ethnic revival belittles genuine social differences between the middle class and poor people. Poor people have no choices. They do not have the luxury of speaking two languages."

I asked Rodriguez whether the absence of Americanist goals to help us through the process of Americanizing a great new wave of immigrants worried him.

"The issue is, what does it take to be an American?" he said. "What is the price? I am not so sure what it means to be a Mexican. I am related to my Mexican ancestors in tone, in gesture, in style. But meanwhile, I have to assert my Americanism, too. You and I, we share the same American air. I have to assert that Abraham Lincoln is my cultural godfather. I have to say that I am more indebted to Jefferson than to Zapata. I am indebted to Walt Disney. Even if I had been taught only in the Spanish language, I would still be forced to be a part of this culture and to know who Farrah Fawcett is. That's why most Hispanics simply become Americans. America is a place where you don't lose your culture—you gain one. Some people have a stake in denying Americanization. But the future already exists. The impact of the Hispanics will not be determined by separatists."

Ever since talking with Rodriguez, I have been thinking that I may have unconsciously aimed my journey at this conclusion, for what he said was what I wished most to hear. He reinforced what I most wanted to believe: that the latinization of America will, in time, lead to Hispanic integration. Whether it will be possible without a fire-next-time, a soul-on-ice, a crisis-in-brown-and-white will be decided partly by the push-pull of Hispanic America into the future, partly by the nature and number of life chances available to Hispanics within the broader society. With Latin America so close by our borders, the melting pot cannot melt newcomers exactly as it once did. But the America of the Hispanics is not the America of our fathers, either. It is bigger, faster, more mobile, more demanding. It may provide patronage, power, and profit, respectively, to educators, politicians, and businessmen who know how to use and promote bilingualism. But it will benefit most those Hispanics who not only speak the English language but also seek a full share in the future of American civilization. The struggle of Hispanics to be integrated involves Anglos as well. "White non-Hispanics" must choose a future, too—as separatists or assimilationists, elitists or Americanists. That is why, I think, it helps to acknowledge that one is an Anglo in the first place: It puts you into the picture. It enables you to see, if you will, that the Hispanic future and the Americanist future can be one. And it positions you for a struggle against the minions of "the new ethnicity"—a struggle that must be made by Hispanics and Anglos together.

Last summer I came across an old Spanish proverb: *Whoever is not called upon to struggle is forgotten by God.* Americans, I believe, have nothing else to fear.

THE HISPANIC VOTE—PARTIES CAN'T GAMBLE THAT THE SLEEPING GIANT WON'T AWAKEN[2]

Within a three-week period in August, President Reagan spoke to Hispanic audiences in Tampa, El Paso, Los Angeles and at a White House luncheon. He also broadcast a radio talk on Central America from Texas, swung south of the border to meet with Mexican President Miguel de la Madrid Hurtado in La Paz and proclaimed the week of Sept. 11 to be National Hispanic Heritage Week.

Announced candidate or not, Reagan's whirlwind courtship of the Latino vote has caused tremors among Democrats accustomed to having that field pretty much to themselves. In early October, House Speaker Thomas P. O'Neill Jr., D–Mass., reacted by blocking action on a major immigration reform bill, saying that he did so because he feared that Reagan would veto the measure to curry favor with Hispanic voters in 1984.

While the premises for the Speaker's action are, at best, highly speculative, there was no questioning his political drift. The Democrats, he declared, "truly represent the Hispanics of America. These are the people my party is trying to help."

At first blush, the attention being lavished upon Hispanics seems disproportionate to their performance in the voting booth. While the 1980 census counted 14.6 million "persons of Spanish origin"—a dramatic 62 percent increase from 1970—analyses of the 1980 presidential election show that fewer than 2.2 million

[2]Reprint of an article by Dick Kirschten. *National Journal.* p 2410–16. N. 19, '83. Copyright © 1983 by National Journal.

Hispanics cast ballots. That was less than 2.6 percent of total turnout, despite the fact that Hispanics are 6.4 percent of the population.

The cultivation of the Latino vote makes more sense, however, when one notes that 94 percent of the 1980 Hispanic turnout was concentrated in nine states that will cast 193 of the 438 Electoral College ballots in 1984.

Within those states, more than two million eligible Hispanic voters were not registered to vote at the time of the last presidential election. For 1984, organizers of an ambitious national Hispanic voter registration campaign hope to add a million new names to the rolls, enhancing the importance of Hispanics as a possible "swing vote" in such populous states as California, New York, Texas, Illinois and Florida.

As demonstrated by the politicking over immigration reform, both major political parties view the potential impact of the Hispanic vote with some apprehension. By tradition, it has been heavily Democratic, but Reagan scored significant inroads in 1980, winning 30–35 percent, according to Election Day exit polls. In 1976, by contrast, Democrat Jimmy Carter won 81–82 percent.

Republicans, hoping that Reagan will run again and at least equal his 1980 performance, have launched "Viva '84," a fundraising campaign with a goal of $1 million for "Hispanic outreach programs and projects." It is headed by Tirso del Junco, chairman of the Republican National Hispanic Assembly.

In an interview, he predicted that O'Neill's tactics on immigration legislation may backfire. Many younger Hispanics are "extremely disappointed" that reforms have been delayed, he said, and that shows "that the Democrats are not looking out for the little guy."

At the Democratic National Committee (DNC), vice chairwoman Polly Baca Barragan applauded O'Neill's "courage and concern for Hispanics" and declared that Reagan's overtures to Hispanics amount to "a lot of rhetoric but no substance." Democratic elected officials, under New Mexico Gov. Toney Anaya, have formed a group—"Hispanic Force '84"—to mobilize Latino voters who Barragan said are "turned off" by Reagan's "insulting" tactics. "They will vote against him," Barragan said, "especially because he puts on his sombrero and especially because he talks about having enchiladas with the Queen of England."

Citizens or Aliens?

A reason Hispanic voter turnout seemed so low in 1980 is explained by William C. Velasquez, executive director of the Southwest Voter Registration Education project, the oldest and largest of three regional groups involved in the national campaign to boost Hispanic participation in the 1984 election.

Of the 8.2 million Hispanics shown by the census to have been of voting age in 1980, approximately a third were "resident aliens," not entitled to vote, Velasquez said. When these noncitizen residents were subtracted, the eligible Hispanic voting age population was estimated at only 5.6 million.

Electoral considerations aside, those figures help explain why immigration reform is seen by politicians in both parties as a volatile issue among Hispanic voters. Simply put, the greatest influx of immigrants—both legal and illegal—over the past decade has come from Latin America. The current Hispanic population is generally thought to be 60 percent Mexican ancestry, 14 percent Puerto Rican, 6 percent Cuban and the remainder primarily from Central America. Of the newly arrived, only the Puerto Ricans are citizens immediately eligible to vote.

Of the sizable flow of illegal immigrants that caused Reagan to remark recently that "this country has lost control of its own borders," roughly half are thought to be Mexicans and another 10 to 15 percent from other Latin American countries. Whatever the exact totals, there are large numbers of persons in the country without the rights and protections that go with citizenship, and a great proportion of them are Hispanics.

The immigration bill now pending in Congress, sponsored by Sen. Alan K. Simpson, R–Wyo., and Rep. Romano L. Mazzoli, D–Ky., entails a dual approach to the problem. It seeks to curb further illegal immigration by providing civil and criminal penalties for employers, whose low-wage jobs are seen as the magnet that draws undocumented aliens across the border. It also seeks to upgrade the status of illegal aliens who are already here.

The Senate bill proposes a two-tier "amnesty" program. Illegal aliens who can prove they have been in the country since Jan. 1, 1977, could apply for permanent resident status and eventually for full U.S. citizenship. Aliens here since Jan. 1, 1980, could seek "temporary resident alien" status, with no social service entitlements, for three years, after which they could seek permanent resident status. After five years as permanent resident aliens, immigrants are eligible to apply for citizenship. Under the more liberal House bill, aliens in the country since Jan. 1, 1982, could apply for permanent resident status.

The House and Senate bills consequently differ significantly with respect to the financial implications of granting amnesty to undocumented aliens, who are not entitled to a wide range of public service and welfare benefits. In July, the Administration estimated that implementing the House bill would cost $11.5 billion from 1984–88, compared with $3.6 billion for the more restrictive Senate bill if that version is amended to include a cap on welfare spending.

Indicating support only for the less costly version, Attorney General William French Smith wrote to the House Judiciary Committee in July that "the rationale for legalization is not to give legal status to *all* illegal aliens but to grant legal status to eligible aliens who have demonstrated a commitment to this country by long-term continuous residence as self-sufficient, contributing members of their communities."

The Senate has passed its version of the Simpson-Mazzoli bill twice—in 1982 and again this year. However, opposition to various provisions in both bills by a coalition of interests that includes major Hispanic civil rights organizations has prevented the legislation from reaching a House vote.

Richard P. Fajardo, an attorney for the Mexican American Legal Defense and Education Fund, said his organization fears that the bill would create a disincentive to hire any Hispanics, legal or illegal. "Employer sanctions would have a severe discriminatory impact upon Hispanics and other 'foreign-looking' individuals," he said.

Fajardo also raised objections to a proposed national identification system, which he said would be necessary to implement the

employer sanctions; to "guest worker" provisions put in the bill
at the behest of agricultural interests that have long been depen-
dent upon cheap foreign labor; and to "loopholes" in the amnesty
provisions that might deter aliens from coming forward to apply
for legal status for fear of being deported if they are turned down.

Arnoldo S. Torres, executive director of the League of United
Latin American Citizens (LULAC), argues that the Simpson-
Mazzoli legislation fails to address the real cause of the immigration problem: the political instability and poverty of the neighbor-
ing nations of Latin America and the Caribbean. "It is false and
irresponsible to claim that this legislation will stem the flow of undocumented people," he said. "Instead, it is Latino-Americans
who will suffer the pain because of our physical and linguistic
characteristics."

Immigration Politics

As political strategists of both parties hungrily eye the 1984
Hispanic vote, the discord over the Simpson-Mazzoli bill poses a
dilemma. On the one hand, there is strong editorial support for
immigration reform in the national press and, judging by the Senate's 76–18 vote in favor of the measure earlier this year, some version of the House legislation very likely would pass with ease if
brought to a final vote.

But leaders—elected and unelected—who purport to speak for
the Hispanic community have almost unanimously condemned
the legislation. O'Neill reportedly developed his own reservations
about the measure after attending a dinner meeting of the predominantly Democratic Congressional Hispanic Caucus on Sept. 15.
At that session, a presentation by Rep. Edward R. Roybal,
D–Calif., detailing Hispanic objections to the Simpson-Mazzoli
bill drew an emotional ovation.

Shortly thereafter, O'Neill announced that he intended to bot-
tle the bill up in the Rules Committee to deny Reagan the opportunity to score points with Hispanics by vetoing it.

Administration officials have denied that a Reagan veto was
ever planned. The President, at his Oct. 19 news conference, said,
"I want to sign, as quickly as possible, immigration reform

legislation." At the same time, he made it clear that his support was for the Senate bill and that he hoped his "disagreements" with the House's version would be resolved in conference.

Despite Reagan's show of support, however, there were some signs of relief at the White House that O'Neill had become the center of the controversy. "It's no secret that we've been hearing from our Hispanic supporters, and I dare say that virtually all of them have expressed concern and, in many cases, opposition to the legislation we've been supporting," said a presidential aide. "It was pretty clear that the thing would cause political problems, [but] they are problems we are prepared to confront, if necessary. Right now, of course, the political situation has greatly changed from what it was prior to the Speaker's action."

O'Neill has been roundly criticized in the press for his action. Rep. Daniel E. Lundgren, R–Calif., who is spearheading a drive to discharge the immigration bill from the Rules Committee, has circulated copies of a telegram in which former Presidents Carter and Ford urged the Speaker to reconsider his decision. For now, however, Lundgren said he has not asked the White House for help in bringing the bill to a floor vote.

Del Junco, the head of the Republican National Hispanic Assembly, believes the issue will turn out to be a big plus for Reagan. A former chairman of the California GOP and a physician in Los Angeles with widespread contacts among that city's large Mexican-American population, del Junco said that he never warned the President about negative repercussions but instead tried to make sure that Reagan was aware of public opinion polls indicating widespread Hispanic support for the bill's basic provisions.

In an interview, del Junco threw down the gauntlet by charging that Democratic politicians such as Roybal are motivated by "other interests," namely business supporters who profit from the status quo. "The people who get hurt [by the existing system]," he said, "are the new entrants to the work force who go to the Hispanic areas and are employed at low wages by the entrepreneurs." He said the opposition to immigration reform comes from "the guys who already are set."

Those, of course, are fighting words to Democratic leaders, who contend that the polls suggesting Hispanic support for the bill are based on questions about general propositions that few would disagree with, rather than on the specifics of the pending legislation. The poll most commonly cited was conducted jointly by Democratic pollster Peter D. Hart and Republican V. Lance Tarrance. Because it was commissioned by the Federation for American Immigration Reform (FAIR), an organization that has lobbied ardently for immigration restrictions, opponents of the Simpson-Mazzoli bill say it should be discounted.

The FAIR poll found, among other things, that Hispanics, by 60–33 percent, favor "penalties and fines for employers who hire illegal immigrants." Among Hispanics who are citizens, employer sanctions were backed by 66 percent. Among those who are not citizens, the sanctions were favored by 53 percent. Another poll, conducted in California by the Field Institute, showed Hispanics favoring employer sanctions by 71–24 percent.

"The question is what kind of questions were asked and how were they asked," responded the DNC's Barragan. "Hispanics, of course, would want fair and just immigration rules. That is something we have wanted for a long time." She added, however, that Hispanics have been conditioned by bitter experience to fear an "overreaction" that may adversely affect people "who may be here legally but have difficulty proving their citizenship because they haven't had good record keeping. You still have that kind of problem in the Southwest."

Barragan, a Colorado state senator whose family has lived in southern Colorado and northern New Mexico for "four or five generations," said that during the Depression, "there were people in the same situation as my family who were put on trains and shipped back to Mexico just because they were poor and spoke Spanish." Rightly or wrongly, she said, such fears are still aroused within the Hispanic community by the current push for immigration reform.

Barragan said that congressional leaders such as Rep. Robert Garcia, D–N.Y., who heads the Hispanic Caucus, should be allowed to develop and propose further refinements to the pending House bill.

Garcia, in an interview, said that caucus members, none of whom serve on the House Judiciary Committee, which has principal jurisdiction over immigration law, will jointly draft an alternative bill next year. If that initiative gains momentum, its base of support may be broadened by the participation of members of the new House Border Caucus, 12 Members from Texas, Arizona, New Mexico and California, all but one of whose districts adjoins Mexico. Freshman Rep. Ronald D. Coleman, D–Texas, who heads the Border Caucus, said he has advised Garcia that his group, which includes three members of the Hispanic Caucus, is willing to help.

Roybal, who developed an immigration proposal of his own and gave testimony before the Judiciary Committee this year, is likely to be at the center of such an effort. In an interview, he said that so far his bill has been ignored. "They put it underneath a big pile of legislation and paid no attention to it," he said.

A Judiciary Committee spokesman countered, however, that the views of Hispanic members were reflected in changes made in the House bill this year, including a substantial liberalization of the provisions for legalizing the status of illegal aliens now in the country.

He added that there is good reason to believe that the bill may come up for final consideration early next year, in which case there would be little opportunity, other than through floor amendments, for members of the Hispanic Caucus to offer an alternative.

Pressure to force an early vote on immigration is coming from Lundgren's discharge petition, which in just two weeks picked up 116 of the 218 signatures needed to bring the bill to the floor.

A Sleeping Giant?

A study of voter registration in New York City, issued in August 1982 by the Institute for Puerto Rican Policy, estimated that two-thirds of that city's eligible Hispanic voters—more than 400, 000 people—were unregistered. The institute, a nonpartisan research organization, described that bloc of unrealized electoral leverage as "a sleeping giant."

To judge by the activities of their national committees, neither the Republicans nor the Democrats appear willing to gamble that the giant will not awake in 1984.

At Republican National Committee (RNC) headquarters, an aide briskly ticked off a list of Hispanic-oriented activities. The committee has its own Spanish-language broadcaster, Carlos Gonzalez-Orellana, who is described as adept at tailoring his phraseology for the diverse consumption of Cubans, Puerto Ricans or Mexican-Americans. With Gonzalez-Orellana behind the microphone, the RNC prepares and offers "radio actualities" for use by 150 Hispanic radio stations across the country. These messages have ranged from translations of Reagan's Saturday radio broadcasts to announcements of Administration accomplishments.

Although the Reagan Administration has cut back federal funds for bilingual education, some agencies, of late, have shown increased interest in the Spanish language. The Office of Personnel Management, for example, announced on Oct. 28 that it "has produced a pamphlet in Spanish for use by Hispanic federal retirees and their survivors."

The RNC publishes—in English—a monthly news report on Hispanic issues called *Focus,* and del Junco's Republican National Hispanic Assembly has its own newsletter, *Boletin,* which recently announced the availability of "Viva Reagan" bumper stickers.

Del Junco explained that "the basis of the whole operation is that the Hispanic community is not homogeneous." He added that the GOP has done "little in the past" to reach out to Hispanics who share the party's views. "We recognize that the two-party system is still around the corner," he said, and added that the party will be well pleased if it captures "anything above 30 percent" of the Hispanic vote.

The Republican appeal initially will be broad, he said, but "the closer we get to the wire, the more pragmatic we have to get"—meaning that additional resources will be directed to Cuban and Central American emigrees, who tend to give more support to Republicans.

At the DNC, which has a Hispanic division as well as its own Hispanic Caucus, there is heavy emphasis on voter registration in the hope of increasing the Democratic vote in states with large electoral votes such as California, New York, Texas, Florida, Illinois, Ohio and Michigan. In a recent report to the party, Barragan said the Democrats' share of the Latino vote was 81 percent in 1976, dipped to 70 percent in 1980 but rebounded to 77 percent in 1982.

A bimonthly Democratic newsletter, *Con Su Voto* (With Your Vote), has been launched, and the DNC expects to offer its own radio and television spots to Spanish-language stations in selected markets. It is also raising a $50,000 campaign fund to assist Hispanic Democratic candidates.

Considerable attention will also be given to showcasing the party's Hispanic elected officials under the "Hispanic Force '84" project led by New Mexico Gov. Anaya. DNC officials proudly point out that cities with large Hispanic populations have chosen Democratic mayors; Maurice A. Ferre in Miami, Federico Peña in Denver, Henry G. Cisneros in San Antonio and Louis Montano in Santa Fe.

The Republicans have mixed feelings about the national Hispanic registration drive, which a GOP official said "is mostly signing up Democrats." Vice President George Bush joined Democratic politicians at the drive's kickoff in San Antonio on Aug. 9, but canceled out of a Chicago rally on Nov. 11. He met instead with Hispanic Republican leaders in Chicago the day before.

That effort, with its goal of registering a million new Latino voters in time for the 1984 election, is in the hands of a coalition of three separate organizations. The Southwest Voter Registration Education Project, based in San Antonio, will conduct 185 local campaigns in the 13 westernmost states. The Midwest Voter Registration Education Project, based in Columbus, plans drives in 50 cities in 10 states from Ohio to Nebraska. The newly formed National Puerto Rican/Hispanic Voter Participation Project will be based in the Northeast and concentrate its efforts on cities with high concentrations of Puerto Ricans, such as New York, Rochester, Newark, Trenton, Boston, Hartford, Bridgeport and Philadelphia.

Juan Andrade Jr., executive director of the Midwest project, said in an interview that the national goal of a net increase of a million in Hispanic registration would probably require that 1.5 million new names be added to the voter rolls. That is because the rate at which Hispanics are purged tends to be fairly high. Andrade said his efforts will center on the large concentrations of Mexican-Americans and Puerto Ricans in Chicago, where a surge in Hispanic registration played an important role in this year's mayoral victory by Harold Washington, a black Democrat. Out of Andrade's 10-state goal of 155,000 new registrations, he is aiming for 100,000 from Illinois.

White House political strategists remain convinced, however, that Reagan is still popular among Hispanics and that the President will once again prove to be an effective campaigner for their votes.

Several recent staff changes at the White House suggest that high-level attention is being given to cultivating Latino constituents. Joseph F. Salgado, a former associate commissioner of the Immigration and Naturalization Service, has shifted to the staff of the presidential personnel office with special responsibility for recruiting of Hispanic appointees. Texan Catalina (Cathi) Villalpando was named in June as special assistant to the President for Hispanic affairs, filling a void in the public liaison office. Her assistant is Jose Velasco, from California, another new appointee.

Over-all coordination of the President's Hispanic strategy is handled in chief of staff James A. Baker III's office by special assistant and fellow Texan James W. Cicconi. In response to suggestions that Reagan's ardor has become warmer as the 1984 election nears, White House aides have readied long lists of events throughout the Reagan presidency involving Hispanics. As an aide put it, "this is one President who doesn't have to be briefed on the meaning of Cinco de Mayo (Mexico's Independence Day). He's been attending Cinco de Mayo celebrations as long as he has been in politics."

Between now and next November, it appears certain that Reagan will not be the only presidential candidate to be observed wearing a sombrero. Whether the Hispanic vote awakens or not, it has the potential to make a giant impact on a closely contested election. If it remains dormant, it will not be because the political parties have ignored it.

HISPANIC VOTE: SLEEPING GIANT AWAKENING[3]

President Reagan travels across the country to have lunch with them. Democratic presidential candidates court them. Hispanic voters, 3.5 million strong and growing, are being hailed as the new power group in U.S. politics.

From farm laborers in Texas and Puerto Rican factory workers in the Bronx to Cuban merchants in Little Havana, Hispanic voters are beginning to feel their political clout.

Their strength, many national Hispanic leaders insist, could very well influence the outcome of the 1984 presidential elections.

"The Hispanic vote could play a big part in the race for the presidency, especially if the race is close," said Harry Pachon, executive director of the National Association of Elected Officials (NALEO), a 2,000-member Hispanic organization.

"It has become chic to court the Hispanic vote," noted Rep. Ileana Ros (R., West Dade). "Politicians have realized that the Hispanic vote was a sleeping giant. The giant is starting to wake up."

Sheer numbers have given Hispanics—the nation's fastest growing minority—visibility in recent years. The 1980 U.S. Census put them at 14.6 million, but Hispanics say their numbers would be closer to 20 million if the estimated 3.5 million to 6 million Spanish-speaking undocumented aliens living in this country were included in the tally.

Some 5.6 million Hispanics are eligible to vote, and they have been doing so with gusto.

Big Increase

There were 3,426,990 Hispanics on the rolls for the 1980 presidential elections, a 30 per cent jump from 2,646,090 in 1976.

By next November, registered Hispanics will be closer to 4 million, according to the Southwest Voter Registration and Edu-

[3]Reprint of an article by Barbara Gutierrez, staff writer. *Miami Herald.* p 6A. Ja. 8, '84. Reprinted with permission of The Miami Herald.

cation Project, a private group that credits itself with registering 100,000 Hispanic voters since 1974.

This new-found interest in the political process has already helped increase the number of Hispanic elected officials at the local level throughout the country.

Ninety-six Hispanics sit in state legislatures. The Hispanic Congressional Caucus swelled from four in 1977 to nine in 1983. And there are at least 12 Latin mayors in U.S. cities with populations larger than 30,000.

In addition, Hispanics recently formed successful coalitions with blacks to elect black and Hispanic mayors in cities like Chicago and Denver.

"Hispanics are excited about the elections," said Mario Obledo, president of the League of United Latin American Citizens (LULAC), the nation's largest Hispanic civic group. "Certainly the spirit is there to make it a record-setting year."

Obledo, along with most other Latin leaders, believes that Hispanics can make a vital difference this year because they could become the swing vote in the states that supply the majority of the electoral votes needed to win the presidency.

Big Bloc

California, Texas, Illinois, New Jersey, Florida, New York, New Mexico and Arizona—all with large Latin populations— hold two thirds of the electoral votes required to reach the White House.

So as Election Day nears, leaders of both political parties are wooing Hispanics with energy.

Evidence: A courting President Reagan traveled to San Antonio and Miami last year, eating tacos and rice and beans in an effort to lure Hispanics to his camp.

Evidence: Leading Democrat Tip O'Neill heeded members of the Hispanic congressional caucus last October and postponed indefinitely the hearings for the controversial Simpson-Mazzoli immigration bill.

"Between Ronald Reagan yelling and screaming about Hispanics' prominence and O'Neill refusing to let the bill out on the floor, we've done more to come of age than at any other time in the United States," said Rep. Bob Garcia (D., N.Y.).

What is crucial now, Latin leaders say, is that politicians pay attention not only to the Hispanic community's new voting potential, but also to its long-standing needs.

Arnold Torres, LULAC's executive director, said his group plans to quiz all Democratic candidates at a February meeting in Washington to which President Reagan has also been invited.

"We are very interested in domestic issues," Torres said. "We want to know exactly what they are offering."

Pamphlet Planned

After the meeting, LULAC plans to issue a pamphlet detailing the candidates' views on topics of crucial importance to Hispanics, particularly immigration, education, crime, civil rights, welfare and unemployment.

The Democratic presidential candidates have already begun focusing part of their campaigns on the Hispanic community. All have named Hispanic liaisons. And both Republicans and Democrats have launched major fund-raising efforts geared to attracting Latin voters.

In "Hispanic Force '84," the primarily Democratic effort led by New Mexico's Toney Anaya, a host of elected officials from all parts of the country are working to register a million Hispanics by election time.

"Viva '84" is the Republican fund-raising campaign that hopes to bring in at least $1 million for Hispanic outreach programs and projects. It is headed by Tirso del Junco, chairman of the Republican National Hispanic Assembly.

Sen. John Glenn has set up "Viva Glenn" clubs across the nation to organize Latin Democrats at the grassroots level.

And Walter Mondale, at a meeting of Hispanic Latin officials last August, pledged his support to help Hispanics raise money for registration drives.

"The Hispanic community has shown an increase in registration and motivation to vote that actually goes against the national trend," said Bill Calderon, Hispanic liaison for the Mondale campaign. "It has become a force for politicians to reckon with."

Less Predictable

Candidates, however, are also aware that Hispanics pose a unique political challenge. Unlike blacks, who are solidly Democratic, Hispanics tend to be less predictable.

Mexican-Americans, who live mostly in the West and Southwest and make up 60 per cent of the Hispanic voters, are mostly Democrats. Puerto Ricans, with 14 per cent of the Latin votes, reside mostly in the North and Northeast and are also mostly Democrats. But the Cubans, who have settled mostly in Florida and New York, make up six per cent of the group and are overwhelmingly Republican.

During the 1980 elections, when 72 per cent of Hispanic registered voters went to the polls, nearly two thirds of them stayed with the Democratic Party. But 80 per cent of the Cubans went for Reagan.

Republican leaders see a trend.

"Democrats cannot take the Hispanic vote for granted anymore," said Jim Brulte, of the Republican Hispanic Assembly.

Congressman Manuel Lujan of New Mexico, a state that has consistently elected Hispanic officials from both major parties, said Reagan could grab 35 per cent of the Hispanic vote nationwide.

"Reagan has finally brought Hispanics the stature they deserve," Lujan said. "He has appointed Latins to places where they've never been before."

But William Velazquez, executive director of the Southwest Voter Registration Education Project, working with the Democrats in the party's registration efforts, said there are natural bonds between the Hispanics and the Democrats.

Natural Affinity

He points out that, except for Cubans, Hispanics have less education, have lower family income and a high unemployment rate and are much more likely to live in poverty than the rest of the U.S. population.

Like blacks, Velazquez said, Latins were sorely hurt by the Reagan Administration's budget cuts.

"That will push them to vote," he said.

Added Garcia, who represents the South Bronx, one of the poorest districts in the nation: "The Reagan Administration has been harsh to our people, to poor people. I think the budget cuts and lack of social services have united Hispanics against Reagan."

Aside from its potential impact on the national election, the 1984 Hispanic vote could also be crucial in a number of local and state races, observers say.

If Hispanic voters in Colorado, Illinois, New Jersey, New Mexico and Texas help elect enough Democratic senators, control of the Senate could be tipped away from the Republicans.

Meanwhile, Hispanic leaders look to a future when a "United Hispanic Front" could promote Hispanic interests in issues such as bilingual education, immigration reform and civil rights.

"If the politicians want the Latin vote," said Tony Bonilla, past president of LULAC, "it's about time they learn to earn it."

HISPANICS' POLITICAL STAR ASCENDING[4]

After the daily noon mass at St. Timothy's in the heart of Mexican-American housing projects on the west side, Delia Lucio stood inside the church vestibule passing out white "power cards." In a few minutes, she had registered 15 new voters.

"I'm going door to door, to clinics, wherever I see people," she said. "The people want to vote. They want to vote Democrat. They know that under the Reagan administration they have suffered badly. I say, well, maybe it's not all Reagan's fault, but maybe it is. I don't know.

"They say, 'This winter, we were very cold.' They paid $150 electricity, $100 rent. What did they have left over to eat? The cuts made it worse and worse. So they come to me and say, 'I want to vote.'"

[4]Reprint of an article by Haynes Johnson and Thomas B. Edsall, staff writers. *Washington Post.* Mr. 25, '84. Copyright © 1984 The Washington Post.

Lucio, a housewife and mother of eight children, is not a political activist in the traditional sense. But she represents a critical factor in the presidential politics of 1984.

In Texas, a vital state for the Democrats if they are to regain the White House, the path to victory lies in the ability of people like Lucio to produce a record turnout of Mexican-American voters in November.

But beyond the clear stakes in this electoral battle lies another, greater political story. It is an old, familiar American one—the rise of immigrant groups to political influence and power.

Now, it's the turn of the Hispanic voters—traditionally more passive and less involved in politics—to follow the path set long before by Irish, Poles, Italians and, more recently, blacks.

Like Americans who trace their origins to Europe, Africa and Asia, Hispanics in fact are not monolithic but culturally and historically diverse—Mexican Americans, Puerto Ricans, Cuban Americans and other peoples with roots in Central and South America and parts of the Caribbean. Yet together they constitute a significant, and increasing, political power, and this election promises to demonstrate their full emergence.

Willie Velasquez, director of the Southwest Voter Registration Education Project, the foremost organization tracking the rapidly changing Hispanic voting population, puts it this way:

"The 1984 election is an excellent time to inaugurate a new era. We used to be concerned about paving streets. Now, for the balance of this decade, we're going to be concerned about U.S. public policy questions.

"After this election people are going to learn about us. The reason we can talk that way is we did our homework at the local level, and that strong political base will produce for us. For us, this is the real beginning of the '80s. For us, the decade starts now."

Hispanics already have rising national political stars, including San Antonio Mayor Henry G. Cisneros and New Mexico Gov. Toney Anaya, both Democrats. Their numbers in Congress are also rising, and should continue to do so with the increase in power at local and state levels.

Hispanic leaders believe history is on their side. They are America's fastest-growing minority and the youngest in median age. With new immigrants arriving daily, and prospect for changes in national immigration policy to permit more Hispanics to become citizens, and thus eligible voters, the Hispanic vote seems destined to assume even greater weight.

Hispanics already are a significant voting bloc in the Southwest—Texas, New Mexico, Colorado, Arizona and California—as well as in New York, New Jersey, Florida and Illinois. But their enormous voting potential has barely been tapped. In 1980, there were 6.6 million Hispanic citizens of voting age, but only an estimated 2.2 million cast ballots. Non-voting Hispanic citizens included 1.1 million in California, 1.05 million in Texas, 467,000 in New York and 206,000 in Florida.

Texas stands as the preeminent example of what can be done. The increase in registration alone has been startling. In 1978 there were 591,950 registered Mexican-American voters here. Four years later, there were 832,000—a 41 percent increase in four years. Nor is the pace likely to slow. At the present rate, the Mexican-American population in Texas will double in 20 years, compared with a doubling of blacks in 33 years and whites in 50 years.

Voting also is rising sharply. In 1976, Mexican Americans cast 278,000 votes in Texas. Four years later, the turnout was 415, 000. This year, with the greatest voter registration drive under way in Mexican-American communities ranging from the big urban centers like San Antonio to rural farm areas stretching across South Texas, the expectation is that 660,000 Mexican Americans will vote.

"Of these, I expect Republicans to get about 15 percent, and it may be as low as 10 percent," Velasquez said.

Republicans, acutely aware of the implications of those figures, are working aggressively to win a larger share in Texas. They say they think President Reagan's popularity will enable them to get as much as 30 percent of traditionally Democratic Hispanic voters.

On the national level, the Republicans are mounting a well-financed, crisply organized effort employing the latest computer technology to identify potential new Reagan voters and get them to the polls next fall.

The national GOP campaign aims at wealthier Hispanics, business executives, veterans and present members of the armed forces. It's especially effective among Cuban-American voters in Florida, where Reagan stirs fervent emotions and voters say their militant anti-communist feelings count more than economic problems when they decide how to cast their presidential ballots. Still, Cuban Americans, who are only 6.8 percent of the nation's Hispanic voters, are dwarfed in numbers and political potential by Mexican Americans.

From 1964 through 1980, Republicans made steady gains among Hispanic voters here and nationwide, capturing 25 percent of that electorate in the last presidential election. It appeared that Reagan's courting of Hispanics was cutting into that traditional Democratic constituency. But two years into his presidency, Hispanic voters turned sharply against him. In the 1982 congressional elections, GOP Hispanic support nationally plummeted to 16 percent and in Texas sank to 7 percent.

Texas Republicans remember vividly what happened just two years ago. A rising tide of Mexican-American voters sounded a bell in the night for the GOP in Texas and set off alarms in the Reagan White House.

The combination of the recession and the rapid increase in Mexican-American turnout defeated the powerful Republican governor, Bill Clements, and put Democrat Mark White in the statehouse.

White won by 231,575 votes. Mexican-Americans gave him 232,379 more votes than they gave Clements.

They represented the margin of victory, and set the stage for the intense voter registration and turnout drive in this presidential election.

"Reagan is very popular with Hispanics middle class and up, definitely," said Byron Nelson of the Texas State Republican Party. "But let's not be unrealistic. He's not going to win majorities. Reagan didn't carry any of south Texas in 1980, and that's the poor, lower-income people in those counties. It is something we are very, very concerned about. Obviously, if we see giant growth trends, then we worry."

At GOP county headquarters here there was no attempt to minimize the difficulty of the presidential effort in Texas. "I think it will be toe to toe," said Brenda Hassel, Republican voter registration chairman for Bexar County.

She added that she had been impressed after seeing how the Southwest Voter Registration Education Project headquarters office in San Antonio was carrying out its massive drive among Mexican Americans. "I was a little sobered," she said, "and wondered whether we would be rolled over by a steamroller."

Republicans acknowledge that they have serious difficulties with Hispanics.

"People come up and ask, 'Why is it that when we go to Republican meetings, we seldom spot a minority face?'" GOP county chairman Knox Duncan said. "If you ask me why the party of Lincoln attracts fewer minorities, I explain that it's a middle-class type party."

Whether 1984 will mark the beginning of a new era of Hispanic political power and influence, as Velasquez believes, remains to be proved on Election Day. But there's no doubt that even at this early stage, an intensive effort is being made to produce the greatest turnout ever and that it already is generating new emotion and enthusiasm. When the Southwest Voter Registration Education Project began a registration drive recently in the valley, 2,000 people showed up in a pouring rain.

Here in San Antonio a number of organizations are coordinating volunteer door-to-door registration efforts at nights and on weekends in the poorer areas of the city. Their goal for San Antonio alone is to register 20,000 new voters between now and the Texas primary on May 5. After that, the goal is to add another 20,000 before the presidential election.

Whatever the future may hold for Mexican-American voters, the present revolves around old problems of poverty, social justice and growing disparities between economic haves and have-nots. That is particularly true among Mexican Americans in south Texas, who were hit severely last winter by harsh weather conditions that ruined crops and raised heating and other bills.

Those conditions bear directly on the election and voter turnout efforts.

"This election is extremely important," said Father Tim Mc-Cluskey, associate pastor of St. Timothy's, a former missionary in South America and presently coordinator of the voter registration campaign for one of the groups here, San Antonio Communities Organized for Public Service.

"For years, San Antonio has been a cheap labor town where people are underemployed or unemployed. I got into this because of the whole question of violence, which came from frustration and unemployment. In the 14 months I've been in Texas, I've buried 23 young people.

"So the issues of jobs and education are forefront in our parish. These are the issues we constantly talk about when we look not only at state elections but national elections."

Sonia C. Hernandez, president of the community organization, also sees the Hispanic voter effort in this area as crucial in November.

"One of our state politicians has said the valley will make the difference in the 1984 presidential election. We extend that. We say south Texas will make the difference."

IV. IS THERE A "JEWISH VOTE"?

EDITOR'S INTRODUCTION

Political commentators often mention the "Jewish vote," implying that millions of people of Jewish origin, living in places as widely separated as California, Florida, and New York, have a single interest and speak with a single voice in elections. Although Jews have formed a part of American society virtually since its inception, the majority of people of Jewish origin are descendants of European and Russian Jews who immigrated during the late nineteenth and twentieth centuries, fleeing, in most cases, from countries whose governments were overtly or covertly anti-Semitic.

The writers in this section argue that, although actual experience, or historical consciousness, of persecution has prompted many Jews to identify with the doctrines of traditional liberalism and espouse the cause of racial equality, the political landscape is now changing and many Jewish voters feel that what *Commentary* calls "the standard liberal agenda" no longer represents their views. Several specific events and developments are named as factors contributing to the debate: liberal sympathies with the Palestine Liberation Organization; the explicitly anti-Semitic tone of remarks by black politicians; and liberal criticism of the policies of the Zionist Israeli government led by Menachem Begin.

The first article, by Jacob Neusner, reprinted from the *National Review,* asks whether American Jews should have a commitment to a particular politician or party and concludes that Jewish secular and religious goals coincide, not with any particular political platform, but with the general good of a pluralistic society. Second, statements from a symposium printed in *Commentary* represent the reactions of a number of Jewish teachers and writers—among them Irving Howe, Sidney Hook, and Seymour Martin Lipset—to a number of questions relating to

Race and Politics

American Jews and liberalism. Finally, Irving Kristol, in a second
article from *Commentary,* describes a sense of "disorientation" in
the Jewish community partly caused by the rise of a new black
nationalism and the breaking up of traditional liberal alliances.

HOW SHOULD AMERICAN JEWS VOTE?[1]

There are half as many Mormons as Jews in this country.
Why don't people write about the Mormon vote at least half as
much as they do about the Jewish vote? Because, conventional
wisdom says, the Mormons are tucked away in the intermountain
West—Utah, Idaho, Arizona. Who cares what happens out there?
But the Jews are spread out in the large and important states of
New York, Illinois, California, Florida, and the like, states which
choose Presidents.

Perhaps so. But perhaps the Jewish vote has become an obses-
sion, something made up by journalists to occupy people in search
of the curious. For Jewish Americans form "the Jewish vote" in
particular when provoked or afraid. Otherwise, they melt into a
variety of other "votes" of which, individually, they form a part:
the union vote, the white middle-class urban vote, the upper-class
liberal vote, the intellectual vote, and the like. To be sure, the stated condition—fear, provocation—turns up more commonly than
one might expect, lending substance to talk about the Jewish vote.
For the walk to the polling place takes a long detour through history. Jews are Jewish by reason of their memories.

What makes a diverse, mobile, highly educated set of people
living mainly in the suburbs of the largest cities of the country,
practicing a wide range of businesses and professions, well represented in government offices, active in unions, visible in journal-
ism, TV, and other parts of the country's communications
industry—what makes these Americans of mainly the third gener-

[1]Reprint of an article by Jacob Neusner, professor of religious studies at Brown University. Reprinted
from *National Review.* p 1250–52. O. 17, '80. Copyright © 1980 by National Review, Inc., 105 East 35 Street,
New York, N.Y. 10016. Reprinted with permission.

ation into "the Jewish vote" at all? And what makes them vote the way they do?

First, of course, there is the State of Israel. You don't have to be Jewish to care what happens to that special place. But if you wonder what life could mean to you if the Jewish state were to go under, you probably are Jewish. The sense of a deep personal tie (short of actually going to live there) is distinctive to Jewish Americans.

Second, there is the memory of the destruction of European Jewry, six million of them among some 15 million European civilians in World War II. An abiding sense of insecurity, an enduring question-mark—these are the psychological stigmata of that awful passion of the Jewish people.

These are special (though not unique). There are general concerns as well. The Jews are mainly a middle-class group, so threats to the order and stability of the country unsettle them. The Jews have learned the lessons of twentieth century history (perhaps later than the Poles or Latvians or Lithuanians, but they have learned). They share the growing foreboding that this country no longer enjoys approximate equality with its enemies. In short, the Jews realize that chaos in world affairs, as at home, is a threat to world order. The absence of a cogent "theory" of foreign policy, the failure of a sense of self and self-interest—these impress this astute and highly educated group. For the lessons of memory favor a stable, orderly community. Jews are victims of mobs, whether mobs in the streets or mobs formed into nations united against them, as at the UN. A strong America, in command of its place in the world, the purposeful leader of a reasoned alliance—that strikes Jewish Americans (in a paradoxical way, to be sure) as a special Jewish concern, even as everyone knows it is everyone's concern.

If these observations seem altogether rational, they are, indeed, too rational. For if the polls are to be believed, it appears that a remarkably high proportion of Jews propose this time around to abandon the two-party system altogether.

Anderson is supposed to exercise a particular appeal to Jewish-American voters. A creature of the mass media, that candidacy, if it attains any measure of success, promises little short of chaos for American politics. The remnants of the institutional support for politics afforded by the two-party system would be swept away in an Anderson victory. What would be left for our system if not a Poujade next time—or a Hitler of 1932? The wheels of the parties grind slow, with their caucuses, conventions, and primaries. But they grind exceeding small. They protect us in their slow deliberation. The whim of the moment is apt to fade away, long before the final choice is laid before the voters. If I had to specify one danger above all confronting marginal people, who must live with the nightmares of pariahs, it is the collapse of the vast, strengthening, stabilizing coalitions of our two-party system. That judgment stands against the present popularity of the *tertium quid*. I think Jews would be wise to pay more attention to lasting institutions and the long-term protection afforded by them.

From institutions we turn to issues. *The* issue—I mean, policy toward the State of Israel—is not going to change many votes. All three candidates have played Going to Jerusalem. The music has not yet stopped. None is apt, before November 4, to find himself without a suitable chair. What happens afterward—who knows? On the one side we have the ritual obeisances. On the other, we have the policies of the years beyond—of 1961, 1965, 1969, 1973, 1977, 1981. Then the music really does stop. En route to Jerusalem, it could be that the Jews will find themselves sitting on the floor. For no one imagines that American policy toward the State of Israel can be governed by a tiny minority of the population, however vigorous and well-organized its support. In the end everyone knows that strategy counts. Nor do Jewish voters want American policy toward the State of Israel to run counter to American interests: they too are Americans.

In this context they listen with special care to the *reasoning* behind the pro-Israel positions. The positions of the principals are for now. But the reasoning (if any) that produces those positions will govern. A pro-Israeli position such as Governor Reagan has outlined, with stress on the strategic value of the State of Israel within the geopolitical frame of America's perspective, in the end will prove more persuasive than assurances added to assurances to buttress an uneven record. For everyone knows that in the affairs of nations there are no friends, only interests, and (as China has shown us) alliances rest upon something other than mere sentiment.

Indeed, a still more compelling issue is whether America's policy toward Israel matters at all. I mean, in the absence of a coherent and encompassing "theory" of the world as a whole, what difference does it make, or can it make, whether the State of Israel is deemed strategically important or peripheral? Absent any strategy at all, it hardly matters. If, further, we lack not only a theory of the world, but a will for our own place in the world, if we swing from this side to that side, explaining the wind as our own will, then who cares what our strategy may be? For it will change, anyhow, when we confront some fresh catastrophe to explain away. Strong support from a weak America, total commitment from a country without commitments even to itself—what use are these to the State of Israel?

But Jewish Americans live *here*. While no candidate indifferent to the State of Israel is apt to win much attention from them, no candidate can have their votes solely by situating himself at the Western Wall. There are concerns at home. These are compelling. Let me take one apt not to be widely understood as special to Jews (as indeed it is not). The American Jewish community has built a massive infrastructure of organizations and institutions. Given the terrible costs of inflation to everyone, I am somewhat embarrassed to point out that inflation also has endangered the entire vast panoply of synagogues, schools, seminaries, fraternal and communal organizations, hospitals, and national organizations, from the center to the farthest fringes. These organizations (and their counterparts everywhere) may be small and peripheral. But they do add up to the inner mode of life for Jewish Americans (as their counterparts do for others). They cannot go on as they have, any more than their counterparts in the other important sectors of American private life can go on as they have.

Inflation has called into question the possibility of a continuing and active life for the private sector of public life. Without the continued prosperity of that private sector, we face the end of countervailing institutions and agencies; we live utterly naked before the all-powerful state. For after all, the state can print money.

But private schools, hospitals, seminaries, fraternal and communal organizations, and all the rest—they can only try to raise it. Ruined by the printing press, they raise it not by collecting taxes from unwilling citizens, but solely by raising contributions from willing donors. But if people continue to face higher and higher prices for basic necessities, they cannot also contribute to the (necessarily) ever larger budgets of the voluntary and service organizations of the Jewish community. (I need hardly add, the same crisis confronts the rest of non-profit and private-sector life in this country.)

What we face at home is the clear possibility of the end of organized Jewish community life. Already inflation has ravaged the cultural life of the Jewish community, with the great national institutions of learning and culture living ever more from day to day. Already the service agencies, such as B'nai B'rith, have had to reduce drastically their services to college students, cut back on their programs in the local communities, and trim to the bone—and into the marrow—even their national staffs.

Inflation is not yet understood as a threat to the ongoing collective life of those important social groups in American society formed around religious, cultural, and ethnic realities. But it is. For without institutions and organizations to give direction and substance to the life of such groups, what is left but inchoate sentiment? A society of shared sentiment, a community of fate, such as Jews make up, goes for nought. Only when woven together with threads of sustaining life—centers and synagogues, philanthropies and inner politics—does the sentiment find substance, the community form and purpose. Once more I stress: inflation counts more important victims than a Jewish school (or a Slovak old people's home, or a Polish social club). But let these lesser victims too be remembered, in the general slaughter of that other structure, the one between the wholly private and the utterly bureaucratic, which Americans, Jews among them, have nurtured through the whole of their history. We are supposed to be a nation of joiners. Inflation will leave us with little left to join.

There is yet another concern at home, captured in diverse ways even though it is one. For Roman Catholics (but not for them alone) that concern is expressed in the symbols of the Right-to-

Life movement. For Evangelicals and other conservative Protestants (and not for them alone) it finds its language in opposition to pornography and reaffirmation of the values of family and home. I am not entirely certain how to phrase the same set of concerns in ways responsive to what is in the troubled heart of the Jewish community of this country. With more than its share among the young folk of the new religions of the day, suffering along with others from the substitution of career and self in place of having and raising children, the Jewish community has yet to find a way to speak to this same sense of a good people and a good society in danger. But the concern is very present and should come to the surface.

The Jews are a very conservative community. They are aging. They are concerned to be able to live in their homes and walk on the streets. They wonder at what they see. They fear. Now you may call this "the social issue," and speak in general terms of family, neighborhood, work. But we Jews have a word which captures much: *menschlichkeit,* a concern for fundamental humanity and decency. No candidate stands against humanity and decency; the two national parties are great because, in the end, they stand for building and maintaining a *menschlich* country.

But when people find themselves called into politics to defend fetal life, to speak in the arena of public policy about family and home, about having children and raising them in a proper and decent way, we must ask ourselves why. I am inclined to look for the answer in the general sense that public policy has provoked the crisis. So the arena of public discourse and political action is the place in which to confront it.

At the outset I questioned the notion of "the Jewish vote." By now I have shown that nearly all elements of the platform suitably addressed to "the Jewish vote" speak to everyone else as well. I see no special Jewish concern for public *menschlichkeit,* for sustaining a society fit for humanity, for finding an ample place in that society for all Americans. I recognize no particular Jewish involvement in the crisis of inflation, for it hits us all equally. I perceive no distinctive Jewish angle on foreign policy, on defense policy, on economic policy, any more than did Jeremiah long ago. He advised the Jews who had been exiled to Babylon in the destruction of the Temple in 586 B.C.: "Seek the welfare of the city where I have sent you into exile, and pray to the Lord on its behalf, *for in its welfare you will find your welfare.*" What is good for America is good for Jewish Americans—equally, and under all circumstances.

A stable, orderly, decent society, with ample place for everyone, and adequate provision for blacks and others with a history of exclusion and oppression; a society in which women have equal opportunity alongside men and in which human life is valued; above all, a society in which people different from the majority are invited to cultivate and enjoy those things which make them different—this is what will win the Jewish vote, and not only in 1980. If I have made a case for Jews to support an essentially conservative public policy, it is because the Jews are an ancient people, with long memories. We have something of more than negligible worth. Ours is the work of conserving it.

LIBERALISM & THE JEWS: A SYMPOSIUM[2]

Recently, the editors of COMMENTARY *addressed the following statement and questions to a group of American Jews of varying political views:*

For many years now, it has been taken for granted by most American Jews that their own interests coincided with and could best be represented through the standard liberal agenda. But this axiom might seem to have been called into question by certain recent developments—the widespread support among liberals for quotas, the diminishing enthusiasm among liberals for Israel, the growing sympathy of liberals for the PLO, and the paucity of liberal pro-

[2]Reprinted are sixteen of the fifty-two responses to *Commentary*'s statement. *Commentary.* p 15+. Ja. '80. Reprinted from *Commentary*, 1980 by permission and by permission of the contributors; all rights reserved.

test against the anti-Semitism that surfaced in the wake of Andrew Young's resignation.

How seriously have these developments affected your own thinking as a Jew about liberalism? Do they warrant a reconsideration by the Jewish community in general of its traditional commitment to liberalism? Do you expect such a reconsideration to take place? If so, is it likely to result in a significant movement away from the Democratic party in 1980?

Elliott Abrams:[*] The state of relations between the Jewish community and conventional liberalism has sunk so low today that the most frequently heard question is "Who deserted whom?" Have Jews become conservative or has the liberal establishment abandoned the liberal principles of the recent past—for example, by supporting quotas and Third World guerrilla groups?

My own view is that liberalism has changed, so that what is now called liberalism no longer holds political liberty and equal opportunity for each individual as cardinal principles. Rather, in today's liberalism a sort of egalitarianism, seeking a leveling redistribution of wealth enforced by constantly growing state power, combines with a curious insensitivity to political repression if it clothes itself in sufficiently progressive—i.e., redistributive—rhetoric. The interests of Jews remain rather stable: we seek to promote the rule of law, political liberty, and individual opportunity, at home and abroad. It is, then, obvious that Jews should find liberalism a bit less winning than in the past. For after all, Jews did not become tied to liberalism out of guilty conscience; we became liberals because liberalism embraced and embodied the political values which protected and advanced Jewish principles and interests. As this ceases to be the case, Jews will find the automatic preference of Left over Right more and more uncertain.

Were Jews simply becoming more conservative, the outcome of these developments would be clear: Jews would become Republicans. And surely this will seem to many to be an attractive option, given standard Republican and conservative views on defense policy, Israel, quotas, and wholesale income redistribution. To the

[*]Elliott Abrams *practices law in Washington, D.C., and writes widely on public policy.*

extent that sentiment alone were to prevent such a development, it would be unfortunate; Jews are not so secure that we can afford to vote against our interests out of sentimental attachments.

Yet to me this option is unattractive, for reasons which go beyond sentiment. If, as I have argued, liberalism has abandoned the old "liberal" principles Jews believe in (and which protect Jews), this will make conservatives appear more attractive *by comparison*. They will be, that is, only comparatively more attractive, without being objectively more so. For the Republican party has over the years shown itself no bastion of support for many things Jews hold dear, such as the struggle for civil rights and civil liberties, and (in no small part through the labor movement) for social justice. To dislike the views of Andrew Young and George McGovern does not mean that those of Jake Garn or Orrin Hatch—or John Connally—are really awfully cozy either.

Which leaves us floating, with the attachment to Democratic-party liberalism broken but not replaced by any real sympathy for the Republicans. But floating is *exactly* where we should be. It is axiomatic that a group whose votes may be taken for granted is a group with limited influence. Were a larger proportion of Jews—larger than the 35 percent who voted against McGovern—to vote Republican in 1980, and were Jews to swing from 80-percent Democratic in one year down to, say, 40 percent in another, the result would be enhanced influence in *both* parties.

I believe this is likely to happen, though not to the extent that interests and principles would seem to dictate. For the sentimental link to the party of Truman and Johnson is strong, as is guilt over appearing "conservative" and thus indifferent to injustice or poverty, and as is the sentiment that Republicans aren't "our kind of people." The GOP, with its flavor of small-town Midwestern business America, holds no comfort for Jews. This is as it should be; parties are shifting coalitions, and it is no more surprising that Jews should become less loyal Democrats than that Southerners or Catholics should be so—all without becoming stalwart Republicans. It is sad, perhaps, but it is necessary; to vote for quotas or against the defense budget by supporting purebred Left liberals is a luxury Jews cannot afford. This realization will dawn on more and more Jews over time, and the Jewish community will be much the better off if it happens soon and is soon understood by the nation's politicians.

Robert Alter: * It seems to me important to distinguish between liberals and liberalism because what has essentially happened over the last decade is that large numbers of those who are eager to be identified as liberals have allowed classic liberal principles to be seriously compromised in the causes and policies they have chosen to advocate. The main reason for this subversion from within of the liberal agenda is obvious enough: the liberal community, whether out of guilt or confusion or still darker motives, has assimilated certain eminently anti-liberal ideas from the radicalism of the late 60's. The most salient of these, at least in regard to Jewish interests, are reflected in the terms of the symposium statement: (1) a rejection of meritocracy in favor of some scheme of "compensatory justice" (racial and sexual quotas); (2) reverse racism (many liberals continue to act in the spirit of Susan Sontag's symptomatic utterance of the late 60's that the white race is "the cancer of humanity"); (3) a rejection of representative government and individual rights as universally applicable ideals in favor of general support for the Third World and its self-styled movements of national liberation, however fanatic, violent and anti-democratic such movements might be.

It hardly needs to be observed that when a liberal agenda begins to encourage discriminatory legislation and a species of racism at home, repressive and belligerent regimes abroad, it has come in its own circuitous way to espouse positions that have been traditionally associated with the political Right. The ascendancy of the Right has always meant trouble for the Jews, and this is no less true when rightist principles are adorned with leftist banners. As a Diaspora community, we depend on a genuinely egalitarian, meritocratic society in which racist attitudes are considered too pernicious to be allowed serious political expression. As Zionists, we know that the survival of a democratic Jewish state in the Middle East requires the staunchest resistance both to the ideal of Islamic regional hegemony and to domination by terror.

* ROBERT ALTER, *a contributing editor of* COMMENTARY, *is professor of Hebrew and Comparative Literature at Berkeley. His most recent book is* A Lion for Love: A Critical Biography of Stendhal.

What is a Jew, or for that matter, any person of liberal conscience, to do about this disquieting erosion of liberalism? The alternatives outside of the Democratic party do not seem particularly encouraging. At this early moment, there is no way of knowing who the Republican presidential candidate will be, but several now in the running might prove even worse for Israel than any Democrat in sight. One should remember that not only Jesse Jackson but also John Connally is prepared to hand over the West Bank lock stock and barrel to the PLO with the demagogic claim that this will bring lasting peace to the region and give America cheap and abundant oil. (It would appear that there are now a dozen motives for Americans to justify Arab militancy, from Third World boosterism to a personal association with oil interests, while there remains scant motive to justify Israel's concern for its own survival.) I suppose the one Republican candidate who is clearly a strong supporter of Israel is Ronald Reagan, but he illustrates all too vividly the danger of trying to choose a candidate on a single issue, for his general views are so retrograde and his competence so questionable that I find it hard to imagine that sane liberals, whatever their concern for Israel, would want to contemplate voting for him.

This leaves us, alas, the Democratic party and the liberal community of America as it is presently constituted. From what I have said, it should be clear that I don't think a reconsideration of the Jewish commitment to liberalism as a political orientation is warranted, and I hope there will be no serious erosion of that commitment. The question, then, is to what extent the anti-liberal positions I have noted are now deeply rooted in the American liberal community, or to what extent they may still be displaced by polemical pressure from within the community itself.

In this regard, I tend, somewhat waveringly, to cautious optimism. The hatred of America and the opposition to democratic values that surfaced in the New Left were deeply felt urges, but the liberal version of such radical ideas is, I suspect, more a matter of vogue, sustained and diffused by the media and the policy-making hierarchies of local and national government. What we may be dealing with, in other words, is ideas that are not the expression of a profound anti-liberal outlook but ideas that have a decade of institutional and propagandistic momentum behind them. This momentum could conceivably be broken by the cumulative shock of external events, like those now taking place in Iran. In any case, I would hope that the growing impingement on vital Jewish interests here and in Israel would impel more and more Jews to speak out against these ideas and to encourage fellow liberals to restore the liberal agenda.

Joel Carmichael: [*] If monotheism is the ultimate source of liberalism, anchored as it is in the universality whose very essence is Jewish, it may seem natural, especially for Jews, to yearn for the realization of a vision embedded in the Scriptures—the brotherhood of man. This ancient connection between Jews and an ideal world would seem to indicate that Jews somehow must be liberal by nature.

Yet essentially this argument generates no more than political extremism. The proclamation of an absolute ideal unaccompanied by piecemeal procedures leading to its attainment is bound to duplicate, in secular terms, the classical religious operation called "forcing the End": the attempt to force God to act is paralleled in the workaday world by the attempt to impose one's will on sluggish history.

No doubt it is obvious that liberal ideals, which can be achieved only approximately, often slip their moorings. Liberals, originally inspired by the desire for a society free of the constraints of authoritarian institutions, often find themselves in practice reduced to the sponsorship of precisely such institutions—notably the state—as long as lip service is paid to ideals.

This surely accounts for the liberal support of wholly repressive agencies like all Marxist governments, and, contrariwise, for liberal hatred of and contempt for free societies that have imperfections.

This strange quirk has its roots in something still more fundamental—the profound alienation that characterizes so many Jewish elites precisely at the pinnacle of success.

Thus the idealistic yearnings typical of so many Jews as they broke out of the *shtetl* a century ago have been magnified still fur-

---

[*] JOEL CARMICHAEL, *the editor of* Midstream, *is the author of* The Shaping of the Arabs, Karl Marx, Trotsky, *and* Stalin's Masterpiece, *among other books.*

ther in their American descendants, the bulk of whom are now solidly established in the middle and upper-middle class. America, too, has numerous shortcomings: an ideal image, even projected onto real societies remote from the individual yearner, is enough to outweigh the merely material and spiritual benefits of a free society, and turns those who enjoy America most into its most insidious enemies.

Thus the split in Jewry that began with the dissolution of the *shtetl* three generations ago has reached what may be a crisis, exacerbated by the rise of the state of Israel as a historical counterweight to the Holocaust.

It is a commonplace for seemingly concerned Jews, precisely, indeed, very Jewish Jews, to refrain, in glee or in sorrow, from sympathizing with Israel because Israel fails to measure up to lofty standards of meritoriousness.

Jewish pathology in this respect is surely unique: no other group will drive its devotion to general principles beyond its own survival. It can hardly be denied that the fine words of liberal idealism often camouflage an attitude of internalized self-denigration on the part of many Jews, whose reaction, precisely in the age of the Holocaust, has been to hide—what could be more natural! And one way of hiding is to choose a universal mask, to avoid initiative, to accommodate, above all, to the aims of others.

This crisis in self-consciousness has now moved into the sphere of practical politics. The activist role assumed by the Soviet executive in the past five years (beginning with the invasion of Angola) has branched out into what is clearly a coordinated campaign of deep penetration, based on the massive use of janissaries from the Cubans to the PLO, and aimed at the exclusion of America from Africa and the Middle East, especially from the Persian Gulf. And as an integral part of the Middle East—indeed, as America's only reliable ally there—Israel's very existence is now in jeopardy.

It is surely a titanic irony that the split of the *shtetl* a century ago should now be influencing world events. It is strange that Jewry, whose role in the destabilization of the Czarist regime was cardinal, should now, after having been crippled in the aftermath of the Bolshevik triumph, espouse in America not merely the principles flaunted by the neo-Bolshevik bureaucrats, but side with the actual regime and its cluster of satellites in their many-sided movement for the extinction of Israel.

Thus Israel, and the free world in general, are now menaced by the Jewish foible for panaceas. In this strange warping of perspective, the indifference to Israel, or indeed even aversion to it on the part of so many contemporary Jewish liberals, plainly echoes the crises provoked in Jewish history by civil-war situations (the resistance to Hellenism, the Maccabees, the genesis of Christianity, the Spanish expulsion).

In argumentation liberals feel virtuous behind their barricade of ideals. At home in the rhetoric of universal aims, they are well-nigh impervious both to practical reason and to the needs of self-preservation.

Yet so many critical situations have been multiplying for the past few years that it seems legitimate to hope that Jewish liberals will change—will perceive the great danger Jewry now faces, very specifically from the forces orchestrated by the Soviet executive. Many Jews, after all, are *not* suicidal: perhaps they may now perceive their historic addiction to panaceas for what it has been—a delusion. If they can be persuaded to exchange their traditional liberalism for a form of it that will enable them to support the true allies of Jews, and in particular of Israel, they will surely find themselves refocusing their world view not delusionally but pragmatically.

All this may be reflected in the upcoming electoral campaign in the United States. Middle East issues are presented to the public lopsidedly, obliquely, distortedly: the range of interests seems endless. Candidates will no doubt be evasive, plausible, deceitful.

Only a sound sense of self-interest can enable American Jews to thread their way between plausibility and sincerity: if self-hatred and self-contempt are hauled out of the unconscious and scrutinized by common sense, those Jews who are basically healthy will, perhaps, regroup.

Arthur A. Cohen:[*] Some time ago, I gave up thinking of myself as a liberal. I have never thought of myself as a conservative.

[*]ARTHUR A. COHEN *is a theologian and novelist whose fourth novel,* Acts of Theft, *will be published at the end of February. His* The Natural and the Supernatural Jew *has just been republished in paperback. Copyright © 1980 by Arthur A. Cohen.*

I have been, as a result, without a tagging device for some time now.

Whatever support I have to give goes to the Western intellectual tradition which has consistently believed that the future depended upon the clarity with which the present estimates the past. My reflective process has, in consequence, always been too slow for political movements. In this sense I think of myself, despite the political requirements of my animality, as an amateur and a proud one at that. I refuse because of the slowness of my ways to be stampeded to the Left or the Right. This does not mean that my position is ever dead Center. I think, as best I can, from issue to issue, and where connections manifest themselves, I allow the move of implication. I generalize about politics reluctantly.

The political scene I find increasingly grim and alarming, less because of a compromised liberalism, willing to make the rush to any and every beleaguered equity, or the Right, increasingly assertive in the development of a politics of national interest, than because the assumption of a reciprocal relation of trust and returned responsibility between the citizenry and the government is eroded. I worry, therefore, about the decline of a presumed moral consensus on which the Constitution and Bill of Rights of this nation have historically relied.

Everything that I have just said is spoken as a citizen of the country, as a second-generation American whose grandparents came from Europe. Those grandparents came from the Hapsburg empire and Czarist Russia. They made it possible for me to be an American, but their emigration did not make it possible for me to be a Jew. Being a Jew is something other and only becomes part of the welter of misunderstanding when a Jew becomes ethnic and quasi-racial. In another context, I have written of this condition as that of the natural Jew, who has interests, concerns, sensibilities not necessarily those of other minorities, but like theirs no less or more privileged. The complexity arises only when the religious distinctness of the Jewish vocation comes to the forefront. The interests of natural creatures, torn by contest and intergroup tension, recede and questions of a destinarian nature reassert themselves. These are questions that implicate the nexus of God, man, and history. They are not relevant here, but they do supply me with a barrier to politicizing ultimate beliefs about the nature and destiny of nations and humankind.

There is little doubt that anti-Semitism has new strength, not only here but abroad, not only in nations with significant Jewish populations but in nations that have only small or remnant communities; neither is there question that black anti-Semitism rises with black frustration, although the latter is no excuse for the former; nor is there question that sympathy for the PLO increases in reaction to the immense cost this country has assumed for securing the Israeli-Egyptian accords and the unwillingness of the Israelis to see their situation the way Americans would like it to be seen. There is a continuous short-circuiting of perception precisely because Americans have been forced to perceive themselves as economically and politically beleaguered, a self-recognition which not even the shock of Vietnam, multiple political assassinations, and Watergate were able to engender. It has taken such bread-and-butter realities as oil, declining exports, the weakening dollar, and unchecked inflation to erode the heretofore olympian confidence of the American middle class. Moreover, no longer a snap of the fingers can put it right. The most powerful nation on earth is not as persuaded by its own rhetoric as it once was. And with all this, it is not surprising—although it is upsetting—that within sectors and pockets of the national community, it is possible once more to speak openly of the world's favorite *bête noire*—the Jews.

On the other hand, I am not certain that even such an interpretation of events would move me as a Jewish American from my amateur preoccupation with social justice and political reform—from my mediate conviction that there is corrigible injustice, that there are still wrongs to be righted, and that even if the poor, blacks, or Arabs turn their backs on me, as a Jew I have at least to understand the predicament of their unreason and their rage before I protect myself and fight back. And beyond this I am more and more persuaded that as a nation we have not yet awakened to the full consequence of the moral disaster of Vietnam, an exemplary model of political stupidity, moral cruelty, and domestic deformation. It might be well for American Jews to underscore rather more than they wish the resemblances between the Germans who invented the death camps and the horrific American ingenuity in Vietnam, lest by denying their metaphysical and moral identity they make it more and more difficult for Americans to recognize and accept their own proper guilt. It is, in other words, easy for anyone to rationalize that all they did was follow orders. As Jews and Americans we have the obligation of sharing with our fellow citizens our understanding of what happens when a nation flees its conscience and what befalls the victims when the moral voice is powerless.

I am not a political analyst, only a political animal, and an amateur at that. I think of my interests but I am not led by them. That, I confess, is mysterious to me. I should be! Most Americans I know allow their politics to be determined by their interests. For some reason I do not. And there are many American Jews I know who are similarly unsynchronized. It has something indubitably to do with the complex interplay of Jewish tradition, conscience formation, and the secular ego, but I am not at all sure how it works. That it works I have no doubt.

It is true, surely, that Jews have been historically voting adjuncts of the Democratic party. I suspect that they will remain so in overwhelming numbers, but why should this change? Should Jews become Republicans because they doubt that the liberal agenda is any longer viable or because they identify that agenda with the Democratic party? And to whom should they turn? Republican promises and prospects are no less fragile than those of the familiar Democratic party, but at least Jews know their way around Democratic politics. Why try and get a berth in a new club, when the old one has their nameplates on front-row seats? Actually, I am being facetious. What I mean is that national debate, national scrutiny of our political order, should take place outside of the party structure. It should be authentic national debate, not party debate. If debate were to take place and if it were conducted with openness, clarity, discernment—in a word, authenticity—it would soon be accommodated to the platforms and deliberations of the parties. (A possible function of television in the national interest might well be such an updated version of *The Federalist* as an instrumentality of instructing and informing the national debate.) However, in the absence of such a national scrutiny—a scrutiny beyond and to the side of parties—it is my view that Jews will again support the candidate of the Democratic party. They may desert the liberal agenda; they might be conservative to their toenails, but it will take some heroic imagining in the Republican party or some well-concerted drive to self-destruction among the Democrats to move Jews out of the party of the New Deal. That's the last time Jews voted their interests and they've not yet forgotten it.

Midge Decter: * In a world full of ambiguities and puzzlements, one thing is absolutely easy both to define and locate: that is the Jewish interest. The continued security—and in those happy places where the term applies, well-being—of the Jews, worldwide, rests with a strong, vital, prosperous, self-confident United States.

With respect to Jews living in the United States, of course, the above proposition ought to be so self-evident as to defy mention. But with respect to the Jews living elsewhere, preeminently Israel and the Soviet Union, it is hardly less so. The Soviet Jews depend on the U.S. to press for and oversee the emigration of those who wish to leave and to keep the Russians at least a little nervous about what they do to those who remain. A U.S. the Soviets did not respect, or let us more accurately say, from whom they felt they had nothing to fear, would now cost many Russian Jewish lives (and many others as well). And as for Israel . . . well, much as one might wish that the Israelis had to depend only on themselves—God knows they have earned the right—it is not to be.

What connection has this to the question of American Jews and liberalism? (Perhaps we should just make a clean breast of things and refer instead to the attitudes and policies of the left wing of the Democratic party, for that is what we mean.) For many years now, the symposium statement says, most American Jews have taken for granted that their own interests coincided with the standard liberal agenda. The story, I believe, is somewhat more complicated than that; permit me to offer my version. For years American Jewish interests *did* coincide with the interests of American liberalism; for that liberalism was in domestic matters

---

*MIDGE DECTER *is national vice president of the Coalition for a Democratic Majority and a senior editor at Basic Books. Her books include* The Liberated Woman & Other Americans, The New Chastity, *and* Liberal Parents, Radical Children.

pluralistic, flexible, committed in principle, and growingly in practice, to large new opportunities for the meritorious—all conditions beneficial to Jews—and in foreign policy committed to strengthening the free world and containing the spread of Communist totalitarianism—it goes without saying, beneficial to Jews and a *sine qua non* for the establishment of Israel. Then two things happened: first, a number of highly privileged as well as highly visible Jews began to feel—it was precisely a mark of their newfound sense of security—that they were now called upon to transcend "mere" interest and be the wise prophets and legislators for mankind as a whole; and second (the exact degree of causal connection between these two phenomena I leave for others to calibrate), the liberal agenda itself began to change. "Change," indeed, is not the word; took a full one-hundred-and-eighty-degree turn would be a better description. Abandoning the old pluralism and flexibility, liberalism, too, became a fount of higher truth and prophecy, truth and prophecy naturally vouchsafed only to those select few who had proven themselves able to adjudicate the needs and rights of others. Domestically, this new liberalism proclaimed that American society was sunk in sin and would be required to make massive atonement, beginning with a denial of both virtue and value to the usual standards of meritorious performance and ending with nothing less than a reduction in the national standard of living. And in foreign affairs, the corresponding proclamation was that the United States was neither powerful enough nor morally creditable enough to continue to play its role as world leader.

Obviously this new kind of liberalism is not in the Jewish interest, and what is more, the Jews all know it. Whatever weakens America weakens them—it is as simple as that. (How this liberal revision got sold to the blacks as being more in *their* interest than the old growth-oriented, pluralistic merit system is a profoundly sad, possibly nasty, and certainly fateful story of our time—but one for another day.) Even those "beautiful of soul," as the Israelis so ironically and so aptly call them, who have "liberated" themselves from concern for the narrow Jewish interest and think instead about love and peace for all mankind, have done so in the serene and self-indulgent confidence that the U.S. will remain rich and strong and that others will look after the dirty details of power for them.

In any case, this new liberalism is bad for the Jews not only because it endorses quotas, has come to extend its highly selective tolerance to anti-Semitism, and regards the PLO (as it once regarded the Vietcong) as a worthy instrument for national self-chastisement. It is above all bad for the Jews because it is bad for the whole country. It has disrupted our delicate civic arrangements, it has distorted our political process, it has undermined our sense of life and tried (unsuccessfully, I believe) to devalue our love of country, it has apologized for crimes against us and our friends, it has taken satisfaction in our humiliation, and it is in general sapping our vitality.

I sense that the "reconsideration" the statement speaks of is already taking place in the Jewish community, no doubt accompanied by some degree of confusion. For among other things, the Jews are losing their home in the Democratic party, a loss that comes hard. Their identification with the old liberalism puts them now in that no-man's-land we call the Center, whose locale, and leadership, has not yet been settled on. I don't think that 1980 will be a problem for them, however. If, as now seems likely, the Democratic nomination goes either to Carter or to Kennedy, I predict a Republican landslide in which the Jews, along with hordes of others disgusted by the spectacle we have lately presented to the world, stoutly take part.

Would such a defection become permanent? Who knows? There is in the offing, if it is not too late, a renaissance of American power. If it comes, when it comes, party won't matter, for it will surely be bipartisan (unless the Democrats wish to commit suicide).

And we will all, Jews at the head of the line, cheer up. And some of us will promise never again to stray.

Rita E. Hauser:[*] In addition to the disturbing developments cited in the questions posed by this symposium, which have surely enforced my prior thinking that the Jewish liberal in America has lost his political bearings, I have found myself for some years unable to answer an even more fundamental question: why has the Jewish liberal been in the vanguard of certain so-called reforms

---

*Rita E. Hauser *is an attorney practicing in New York City and a prominent Republican.*

which, if enacted, would serve to diminish most considerably the influence American Jews could bring to bear on the political process? If American Jews collectively were stripped of political power, then it would matter very little indeed where they stood on any issue since, *in toto,* Jews represent a small percentage of the total voting electorate.

The first such "reform" has already been felt. The limitation on campaign contributions in federal elections to $1,000 per candidate has eliminated the strongest weapon the Jewish community exercised in influencing the selection of nominees in both political parties. John Connally could risk alienating Jewish Republicans by a profoundly anti-Israel position taken very early in the campaign season because, among other things, there were no heavy Jewish contributors weighing in, as was the case in the Nixon and Ford campaigns. Jewish liberal "reformers" were in the vanguard of those who supported this limitation on campaign contributions, perhaps ashamed of how money, yes, Jewish money, could count in the precarious days which mark the beginnings of any candidate's venture.

Jewish liberals have also been in the forefront of those seeking, happily without success thus far, to eliminate the electoral college and replace it with a one-man/one-vote system which would reduce Jewish interests and issues for any presidential candidate to a bare minimum. Jewish votes matter because Jews are concentrated in states with the highest electoral count and, in a tight national election, such as the Ford-Carter race, a swing of just 1 or 2 percent of the Jewish vote is the difference between victory and defeat. No presidential candidate in 1980 can afford to alienate a sizable percentage of the Jewish vote since there is no way he can win what will surely be a close election without a minimum 20–25 percent of this vote in the key states.

Jewish liberals who support these "reforms," who excuse black anti-Semitism, and who argue for a PLO-dominated state on the West Bank, must somehow believe they, and Jews in general, will be rewarded for their "good deeds" and moral stance at such time when Jewish political power in America is insignificant and when Israel will be in a position of strategic weakness. Since history teaches that political reality denies influence to those who are unable to exercise it, Jewish liberals who work for the diminishment of Jewish political power are dangerous people indeed. Many clear-headed Jews have moved away from such folly and now are able and willing to support Republican candidates, as well as more conservative Democrats. They understand that the first commitment of Jews today is to Jewish survival, and not to any outmoded dogma which does not seek to insure that aim. An intelligent Jewish voter really asks himself first and foremost that ancient question, "Is it good for the Jews?" Many Jews did not like Nixon, but in view of their perception that McGovern was indeed bad for the Jews, bad for Israel, and bad for America, over 35 percent of them voted for Nixon in 1972. Despite Watergate, if that election were replayed today, the outcome, in my opinion, would be the same. Most Jews are intelligent enough to know that the standard liberal agenda no longer serves them well.

Arthur Hertzberg:[*] From its beginnings two centuries ago in the era of the French revolution, liberalism has meant at least two things. It has contained a reformist majority and a doctrinaire left wing. In the 19th century, the heirs of Montesquieu and the Gironde became social democrats. Those who looked back to Robespierre and the Jacobins became revolutionary socialists.

Not every reformer in the last two centuries has liked Jews or wanted to help them increase their role in society, and many revolutionary socialists, such as Lenin, have fought against anti-Semites both of the Right and of the Left. Nonetheless, on balance, the revolutionary Left has had a marked and lasting tradition of imagining a new heaven on earth without Jews. The emancipation of the Jews, wherever it has occurred and has lasted, has been the work of centrist liberals.

A comparable analysis could be made of conservatism. Both English Tories and the Black Hundreds of Czarist Russia are termed conservatives, but there is a vast difference between ideologues who engage in repression and an aristocracy, such as the British, which sometimes "dished the Whigs" by moving over to accommodate new forces which might otherwise make revolution.

[*]ARTHUR HERTZBERG *is rabbi of Temple Emanu-El in Englewood, New Jersey and was president of the American Jewish Congress from 1972 to 1978. His most recent book is* Being Jewish in America.

We are not now hearing of comparable tensions within liberalism for the first time in America. The Communists and even Norman Thomas, the leader of American socialism, remained in the 1940s doctrinaire opponents of Zionism. The political and religious Left of today did not invent the rhetoric of anti-Zionism; it was to be found in the *Christian Century* of the 1930s and 1940s, against which Reinhold Niebuhr fought. The concreteness of Jews in their own right, which includes the commitment to Zionism and the economic profile of a group largely concentrated in managerial and professional roles, was attacked and reattacked a generation ago by people as diverse as Henry Ford and Father Coughlin; Jews are now attacked by both John Connally and Jesse Jackson.

Neither conservatism nor liberalism, if each is defined at its most extreme as a movement of either the revolution or the counterrevolution, is the political home for Jews. Jews have flourished best in Anglo-Saxon countries, in Britain and its former colonies, and, of course, in the United States, where an expanding capitalism, for which an untidy liberalism speaks, has made room for the rise of Jews into society.

What is most significant in America today is that, contrary to the phrase from Yeats that is so often quoted, the Center is holding. It is the task of Jews, for the peace of society and for their own sake, to help it hold. Jews—and fortunately not they alone—are working to find the middle ground. So most Jews are rightly for neither "affirmative action" nor the equally dangerous assertion that only "merit" must prevail. The most recent Supreme Court decisions have been muddled and not very satisfying. In that very muddle, there is more sense than in any clear-cut victories for one or the other side.

The unideological Center of American life remains committed to Israel, not as either a permanent forward bastion of the cold war or a permanent occupier of the West Bank. The mainstream of American opinion is no different from the Jewish consensus, both in Israel and the United States. Here, too, the ideologues of the Right and of the Left, Islamic Marxists, black nationalists, Gush Emunim, and so on, demand clarity based on their unvarying absolutes. There is no balm for Gilead in any of these doctrines, only in untidy accommodations.

In American politics Jews will no doubt remain largely in the Democratic party, but it is not unhelpful that there is a substantial representation now among the Republicans. In both camps, the weight of Jewish opinion and activity is in favor of the centrists.

There are, of course, Jews who find this discomforting. They prefer to dream dreams and see visions of a new world in the creation of which a Jewish political intelligentsia plays the priestly-prophetic role. Most Jews have, however, learned that Trotskys may serve the revolution of the Left brilliantly, but Jews are ultimately not safe within it. Comparably, the right-wing rulers of inter-war Poland did not protect their Jewish friends, even those who were, there in the 1920s and 1930s, the intellectuals of the Right.

America is today facing two fundamental problems: how to accommodate to a changed, and probably reduced, role for itself internationally and how to reorder its society to accommodate what is an increasing microcosm of the white-Western/Third World encounter.

For Jews to be on doctrinaire barricades on either side at this moment is to help increase the tensions and to run the danger of being swept away if the confrontations, especially the domestic ones, become sharper. America as a whole no longer controls events abroad. The Center must be made to hold at home.

Milton Himmelfarb: The political scientist William Schneider's summary of the facts rules out interest ("life situation") as an explanation of Jewish liberalism:

Jewish voters are typically *more* liberal and *more* Democratic than any other (white) ethno-cultural groups . . . even more distinctively Democratic than blacks. Blacks vote "with" their life situation: they vote Democratic because they are poor and they vote more Democratic because they are black. Jews vote "against" their life situation.

*Milton Himmelfarb, *a contributing editor of* Commentary, *is the editor of the* American Jewish Year Book *and the author of* The Jews of Modernity.

When the "Statement Unanimously Adopted by [the] Black Leadership Meeting" last August dismissed the Jews' liberalism as rooted in "their perceived interest," the black leaders had their reason for saying what they said. We have no reason to add to the obfuscation. How was it more in the interest of Jews than of Italians, Poles, Seventh Day Adventists, or Mormons to support desegregation of the schools or to send a check to the NAACP?

The black leaders' assertion of a Jewish interest is like that easy refutation of altruism: "Superficial people call an act altruistic when it seems not to be in the interest of the actor, as when he gives money or undergoes hardship for the benefit of others. Nonsense. The seemingly altruistic act makes the actor feel good. That is his reward, and where there is reward there is no altruism." It is by definition, therefore, or rather by tautology, that Jewish liberalism springs from Jewish interest. The black leaders stated without apology that blacks act in their own interest. That is the American way. An odd consequence is that of all American Jews the Hasidim of Brooklyn are the most American in their politics.

In a 1978 Harris poll for the National Conference of Christians and Jews, 39 per cent of "national black leaders" thought "Jewish groups" really wanted to promote "black equality"—more than thought the Catholic Church did (37 per cent) or white Protestant churches (6 per cent). Ordinary black respondents gave Catholics 25 per cent, Jews 18 per cent, and white Protestants 12 per cent. Now comes the shocker. Asked whether, "when it comes to choosing between people and money, Jews will choose money," 56 per cent of ordinary black respondents agreed—8 per cent more than in 1974. That is bad enough, but not so bad as the response of black leaders. Of these, the very people who thought Jews better disposed than other whites to black equality, 81 per cent said that Jews will choose money over people: four out of five. Asked whether "most of the slumlords are Jewish"—not some, or even many, but most—37 per cent of ordinary black respondents said yes in 1974, and 41 per cent in 1978. In 1978, 67 per cent of black leaders said that most of the slumlords are Jewish: two out of three. With such friends, who needs enemies?

A realist knows that if you don't want someone to dislike you, you don't do him favors. (Give one man a job, according to the politicians, and you make ten enemies and an ingrate.) A realist would say that if we had acted from interest and not done favors for black leaders they might now dislike us less or, better still, have us on their minds less. Hispanics—Puerto Ricans, Mexicans, and so on—are taking over from blacks as the biggest and most clamant minority. If we learn from our experience with black leaders, we will not do favors for Hispanic leaders. But we will not learn. First we will do them favors and then they will say we did the favors only because it was in our interest to do them. And what have we done for them lately? Besides, everyone knows that most of the slumlords are Jewish.

We will not learn because we do not want to learn.

If our rote liberalism has been against our interest, it does not follow that rote conservatism would be in our interest. It is in our interest to feel free to vote for one party or the other, and especially to be seen to be free. It is further in our interest that we should be enrolled in each party in such numbers as to discourage stands damaging to us. What is Connally's strategy? First things first— before he can be elected he has to be nominated. He does not expect his anti-Israel position to hurt him in the primaries. On the contrary, he expects it to help him, if only by setting him off from the other candidates and making him seem bolder and more forthright. So he offends Jews. What does that cost him? Everybody is a little annoyed with us, and there are not enough of us voting in Republican primaries for him to worry about. He can cozy up to us later. But even then, how much thought will a Republican nominee give to the Jews? Goldwater said a nominee hunts ducks where the ducks are, and Republican ducks are not Jews.

Before the 1972 election there was hardly an issue of a news magazine without its revelation about the new Jewish conservatism. Though the Democrats were then, as now, the majority party, and though the Republican nominee was unattractive, about 69 per cent of white Christian voters voted against the Democrat. Of Jewish voters, about 65 per cent voted *for* him. That is what Jewish conservatism means: giving a two-thirds vote to the most unpopular Democratic candidate in memory. Compulsive smokers know that smoking is not good for them but they keep smoking. Most Jews are compulsive Democratic voters. As a friend of mine puts it, "I'm an independent, I always vote Democratic." A sensible Republican is unlikely to put great effort into hunting such elusive prey. A sensible Democratic candidate is unlikely to put great effort into winning over people who have shown that they will vote for him regardless.

What partially saves us, in spite of ourselves, is the importance of a swing. Since one Democrat who votes Republican is worth two votes to the Republicans, the one that they got and the one that the Democrats lost, it does make a little sense for Republicans not to give up on the Jews completely and for the Democrats not to take us for granted completely.

Mayer Amschel Rothschild had one son in Germany, one in Austria, one in Italy, one in France, and one in England. No matter who won in a warring Europe, the Rothschilds would not lose. But then, in those days the religion of most Jews had not yet been superseded by Progress, a.k.a. Liberalism.

Sidney Hook:[*] It would be a profound error for Jews to forswear their allegiance to the social and political philosophy of liberalism because some erstwhile liberals have betrayed its fundamental principles. Those of us who have condemned the quota system and especially the outrageous decisions of the Supreme Court in the *Weber* and *Bakke* cases have done so because they violate what until now has been regarded as axiomatic to a liberal philosophy and not because of the adverse consequences of quotas for Jews or any other group. We would just as vehemently oppose a quota system that favored Jews.

There are few propositions that are demonstrable about human affairs. The nearest to one is the view that those who desire to preserve their individual or group identity as Jews are more likely to do so without suffering official persecution in a community governed by liberal principles than in any other. This is not the only or even the chief reason for adhering to the liberal faith. The grounds on which one holds a liberal philosophy, if valid, justify

[*] SIDNEY HOOK, *professor emeritus of philosophy at New York University, is currently a senior fellow at the Hoover Institution, Stanford University. His books include* The Hero in History, From Hegel to Marx, *and the forthcoming* Philosophy and Public Policy.

commitment to it not only by Jews but by reasonable men and women regardless of their color, sex, creed, or national origin.

The issues involved in this discussion are old, perhaps one should say perennial. It probably testifies to my limitations, but I cannot see in what way the position I advanced in an article in the *Menorah Journal* in the fall of 1937, "Promise Without Dogma: A Social Philosophy for Jews," has been rendered anachronistic by events since then—except possibly in one respect. I argued at the time that the conditions a social philosophy must fulfill "to be acceptable to Jews who wish to survive, of course, not exclusively as Jews, but as Jews nonetheless are (1) a recognition of the value of cultural diversity; (2) tolerance of religious differences; (3) a fighting faith in democracy as a way of political and social life; (4) acceptance of an ideal of economic reorganization which, for want of a better name, I would call democratic socialism; and (5) reliance upon the methods of critical inquiry in approaching all problems." The one respect that requires modification was expressed by Alvin Johnson in his eloquent and vigorous response to my article in the subsequent issue. Agreeing with most of what I wrote, he took issue with my fourth criterion: "I will go farther and assert that there is no hope for the Jew as Jew in socialism, if by socialism we mean an economy organized as a single unit, centrally controlled and managed. No matter how liberal might be the constitution of a state that set itself up as an exclusive employer, that controlled all the avenues to a living, the exigencies of technological operation would force it along the path of totalitarianism."

Actually at that time, like most socialists, we envisaged something far short of a completely collectivized economy. The customary reference was to "the commanding heights" of the economy. Later, following the lead of Norman Thomas and John Dewey, we set our political sights on the development of a genuine welfare state with a mixed economy. But we were remiss in not grasping sooner and more vividly the totalitarian potential of the Soviet model of economy not only for Jews but for all human beings enmeshed in its operation. Events have made Alvin Johnson's warning more prescient.

Irving Howe:[*] Let's glance at the reasons COMMENTARY gives

[*] IRVING HOWE, *the editor of* Dissent, *is the author of* The World of Our Fathers, The Decline of the New, *and* Politics and the Novel, *among other books.*

for calling into question the "axiom" of Jewish support for liberalism:

"Widespread support among liberals for quotas." In some instances, no doubt. But more widespread, I'd say, is liberal support for affirmative action, something to be seen as decidedly different from quotas. This distinction is habitually denied or minimized in COMMENTARY: but many distinctions are habitually denied or minimized in COMMENTARY. I can hardly suppose that supporting affirmative action makes one an opponent of Jewish needs, otherwise it would be necessary to condemn a good many Jewish organizations that can not be described as radical.

"Diminishing enthusiasm among liberals for Israel." No evidence being offered, it's hard to know what COMMENTARY has in mind. The one major instance of such "diminishing enthusiasm" in American political life has come from John Connally, representative of Texas oil and corporate America. What can, however, be said is that many liberals—and American Jews as well—are greatly disturbed by the Begin government's evident intention to maintain its domination over the West Bank and the Arabs who live there, an intention that violates the democratic ethos (and threatens the Jewish character) of Israel. To criticize these Begin policies from an appropriately pro-Israel commitment seems to me not a sign of diminishing enthusiasm for but an act of urgent defense of Israel.

"Growing sympathy of liberals for the PLO." Possibly so, among some. But mostly what I see, out there in the real world, is a recognition—often reluctant and unhappy—that a Palestinian national sentiment is now a historical reality not to be dismissed by looking the other way and that a final peace in the Middle East will have to cope with this reality. Not just the unnamed liberals COMMENTARY invokes but an increasing number of Israelis and even some American Jews are being driven to this recognition, and it has nothing whatever, certainly nothing necessarily, to do with "sympathy" for the PLO, either its ideology or methods.

Now, none of this is to deny that the liberalism of at least some American Jews has become less assured, more troubled and qualified. Of course; but it hardly distinguishes them from other Americans. As we now enter a new stage, or resist entering a new stage, of the welfare state, liberalism is experiencing a severe intellectual-political crisis. This crisis is partly a result of its own (limited) successes—the achievements of the welfare state in which we live. It is partly a result, also, of its own failures—the difficulties of coping with unforeseen or underestimated problems of the welfare state. And it is partly a result of the inner hesitations of American liberalism to recognize that the first initiating phase of the welfare state having now been more or less completed, it's necessary to move toward a modestly radical or social-democratic policy that would signify a stronger egalitarian commitment and a sharper threat to corporate hegemony. Liberalism today is roughly in a stage similar to that in which it found itself during the decade before the New Deal: regathering intellectual energies, working out new programs, fending off attacks from enemies and fading friends. I believe that with an increment of social-democratic policies in the economic sphere liberalism will again be resurgent at some point in the 1980's and that many American Jews will contribute significantly to this event.

But surely there are also special "internal" reasons for the weakening of liberal attachment among American Jews and here I can note only a few:

It may be—proof would be hard to come by—that the improved socioeconomic position of some American Jews is gradually having its political impact. Jewish commentators have often stressed, with pride and/or regret, that when American Jews move up the socioeconomic ladder they do not, like other groups, become more conservative but retain their liberal attachments. Just possibly—this is my impression from traveling about the country—the slow process of "normalizing" our socioeconomic position has begun to produce some unattractive "normal" consequences.

The pressures of the Begin government even in its brief tenure have led to a notable turn toward chauvinist sloganeering among portions of the American Jewish community and an increase of uncritical responsiveness to whatever signals come from Israeli spokesmen. To be fair, this had already begun under the Labor regime, e.g., Rabin's not very subtle nods toward Nixon.

An odd paradox characterizes American Jewish institutional life, namely, that such leading journals as COMMENTARY and *Midstream* appear to be somewhat, perhaps a good deal, more conservative than their sponsors. Many American Jews probably don't know that major Jewish organizations, including the American Jewish Committee, while opposed to quotas, have come out for affirmative action, and they may suppose that the campaign of COMMENTARY to meld quotas and affirmative action represents a unified Jewish opinion. Those of us who disagree sharply with COMMENTARY's line must be realistic enough to admit that it has had an impact upon the thinking of Jewish institutional spokesmen, perhaps by hardening impulses already there.

A withdrawal of Jewish commitment to liberalism would be a disaster for the country and also, I think, for the Jews. A large segment of American Jews—the professional and semi-professional classes—is deeply enmeshed in the workings of the welfare state and has an economic and intellectual stake in its flourishing. More important, even if one wished (or thought it possible) to withdraw to a parochial "interest-group" view of Jewish life, it could still be strongly argued that staying with the universalist vision—a belief in a liberal society of steadily-accumulating social reforms—remains the best way of defending strictly Jewish interests and an important way of sustaining the inner morale of the Jewish community. But most important, social liberalism has been defined as the "secular religion" of many American Jews, the precious salvage from their immigrant and East European heritage, the embodied value of a major segment of Jewish experience. That in the long run even this liberal commitment might not suffice, at least by itself, to maintain a vital Jewish presence in America could be cogently argued from an Orthodox or Conservative religious position. But that is not the standpoint from which COMMENTARY asks or answers its questions. If we tacitly agree, then, to remain largely within the secular realm, I think it all but self-evident that liberalism still offers the best (though not an unmarred) framework for the effort to realize humane values—freedom, egalitarianism, fraternity—in the society at large and to assert the validity of specifically Jewish claims. The case for Israel, to cite one crucial example, is far more strong-

ly made in terms of its democratic character and historic ties with
Holocaust survivors than in the shaky categories of American
"national interest."

I am not saying here that liberalism is "inherent" in Judaism
or that the Prophets were canny enough to anticipate my politics.
But as a democratic socialist who cares about Jewish values, I continue to believe that liberalism is our natural home, insofar as we
can ever be at home. That is why I oppose the extremist conservatism that has recently flourished in the pages of COMMENTARY and
that is why—it's not a matter of personalities or literary feuds—
we may expect a hard political-intellectual battle within the Jewish arena during the next decade. Meanwhile I thank the editors
of COMMENTARY for granting me this space to express my opposition to their views.

Seymour Martin Lipset: * Has the vaunted commitment of
Jews to Left and liberal causes ended? A myriad of articles has
sought to describe and explain a shift to the Right among Jews,
supposedly linked to conflicts with other minority groups and
women activists over affirmative action; to an awareness that those
more disposed to the Left are also more anti-Israel; and, on a
higher, more philosophical level, to the recognition that Jews have
a stake in a stable, legitimate social order. The more cynical or
Marxist-oriented analysts account for the supposed change by
making the assumption that the wealth and high socioeconomic
status of American Jews press them to bring their politics into line
with their privileged class position.

These interpretations are logical, but they have one fault—
they do not fit the facts. Studies of Jewish attitudes and political
behavior continue to find that Jews remain the most liberal white
ethnic or religious group in the nation. A late November Gallup
release reports that Edward Kennedy, accurately perceived by the
populace as the most Left or liberal of the candidates, has a larger
lead over Carter among Jews (64-16) than among any other group
of Democrats, including blacks and Kennedy's fellow Catholics.
Analyses of voting behavior find that American Jews remain more
committed to the Democratic party than any other ethnic or reli-

*SEYMOUR MARTIN LIPSET *is professor of political science and sociology, and a senior fellow of the Hoover
Institution, Stanford University. He has just edited* The Third Century: America as a Post-Industrial Society.

gious group, except for blacks. Within the party, as their current presidential nomination preferences indicate, Jews are the segment most disposed to back the more liberal, New Politics wing. In 1972, when McGovern's dovish views were supposedly alienating pro-Israel Jews, he secured about two-thirds of the Jewish vote, more than he received from any other white group. In June 1978, a small majority of California's Jewish voters opposed Proposition 13, while 65 per cent of the electorate favored it, according to a Los Angeles *Times* survey. In November 1978, 69 per cent of the Jews voted for Jerry Brown for governor, a far higher percentage than Brown received from Catholics and Protestants. In the 1978 congressional elections, 72 per cent of the Jews queried as they were leaving polling places told New York *Times*/CBS interviewers that they had voted for Democrats, in contrast to 60 per cent of the Catholics and 45 per cent of the Protestants. Only 16 per cent of the Jewish voters described their political views as conservative, compared with 27 per cent of Catholics and 37 per cent of Protestants.

The same New York *Times*/CBS survey found, as of election day 1978, that Jews were more dovish on issues of foreign policy and defense expenditures than other ethnic or religious groups. Surveys conducted by different pollsters throughout the 70's have reported that Jews are far more liberal than others on social issues, e.g., abortion, premarital sex, civil liberties for dissident views, the rights of homosexuals, and, most surprising of all, affirmative-action, special-preference programs. Proportionately, Jewish backers of affirmative action/quotas outnumber those in the various white nationality and religious groups, but on this issue alone they lag behind blacks.

Much of the impression of growing Jewish conservatism has come from the attention given to the views of prominent Jewish intellectuals who have moved from earlier leftist commitments to ones which have been described as neoconservative. In fact, most members of the group so labeled are Democrats and relatively liberal on domestic issues. A few even describe themselves as socialists or social democrats. And in any case, massive surveys of academic opinion taken in 1969 and 1975 by the Carnegie Council Commission on Higher Education indicate that Jewish faculty, who number around one-tenth of all American professors, are far more liberal than their Gentile colleagues.

A great majority of the Jewish public and intellectual elite has remained very liberal on most social and economic matters and in its voting behavior. This conclusion may be countered by the support given to a few moderate Democrats, like Senators Moynihan and Jackson, who are highly visible and important backers of Israel; by the endorsement of a hard-line foreign policy by the small group of "neoconservative" intellectuals; and by the voting behavior of less privileged and more Orthodox Jews still living in high-density urban areas who have backed hard-line law-and-order candidates in local elections. But the more numerous affluent segment of the Jewish community continues to opt for liberals locally as well as nationally, and constitutes the most important source of finances for liberal and Left causes.

What still remains unique about the politics of American Jews is how liberal-Left they are after having become one of the most affluent ethnic-religious groups in the nation. It is the continued liberalism of the Jews that should be commented on and explained, not their relatively minimal drift to the Right.

Edward Shils: [*] The "interest" of Jews in America can be very variously defined. For those who are ambitious, equality of opportunity in every field of activity regardless of religious belief or affiliation or ethnic and religious ancestry is a desideratum. For those who wish to live according to the law, the freedom to do so without suffering any disabilities other than the inconvenience which this necessitates in a society in which they are a small minority is to their interest. For those who wish to divest themselves of their traditions and to be nonbelieving, nonobservant Americans of Jewish ancestry, the freedom to do that without having their ancestry held against them is to their interest. These "interests" of the Jews have existed ever since they came to the United States. Many of their civic activities have been formed about these interests, the satisfaction of which required the continuation and extension of the liberalism already widely practiced in many parts of the American society to which they came. Other

---

[*] EDWARD SHILS *is a member of the Committee on Social Thought and professor of sociology at the University of Chicago. His most recent book is* The Calling of Sociology.

contemporaneous immigrant groups had similar interests, but since they were not so ambitious as the Jews, they did not perceive these interests so urgently.

The American Jews thus had interests in common with all other Americans, which were to maintain and protect a liberal society. In this same sense they also had interests in common with blacks who were not recent immigrants and who wanted to have the same access to opportunities and rewards as persons of the prevailing type of pigmentation. For some reason, the Jews active in the main Jewish civic organizations became patrons of some of the main black organizations which were seeking to improve the civic and economic conditions of the black within an American society which they accepted in principle. The blacks, like the Jews and other recent immigrant ethnic groups, had an interest in being judged by those in authority in institutions in accordance with criteria which referred to their capacities and conduct and not to their pigmentation, or their present or ancestral religious beliefs, their recent territorial provenance, or the occupations of their ancestors.

The Jews' real interest, as Americans and as Jews, was above all to maintain American society as a liberal society of human beings as free as stability and orderliness allow, and to respect the traditions of national loyalty in which their fellow countrymen lived and which were essential to their society's liberalism. There were some points of conflict between their interests as Americans and their other interests as Jews. There were points of conflict with some of their fellow Americans, who were not as liberal as they were under obligation to be. There were also points of conflict because some of the Jews were not always as liberal in certain respects as the maintenance of American society required; they came to think that American society had to be fundamentally changed. They inclined toward the revision of liberalism in the direction in which a handful of American intellectuals, academics, and publicists, and a few politicians, were already trying to change it. As it has turned out, these changes were not changes in the direction of an extension of liberalism. Nonetheless, the proponents of these changes claimed to be liberals, although the program which they espoused came from a very different tradition, the tradition of adulation of the state, the tradition of *Kathedersozialismus*. This belief in the omnicompetent, omniprovident government has in the United States taken the form of collectivistic liberalism.

By and large, the first generation of American Jews of the great immigration which ran from the 1880's to the beginning of the second decade of the 20th century, jettisoned more of their own Jewish traditions than they needed to in order to gain what they desired in and from American society. In the difficulties under which they had to labor, as poor, uneducated, and newly arrived, they did quite well what they had to do. They were not political philosophers and they knew nothing about the doctrine of liberalism. Nonetheless, they became liberals. Some of them also slipped easily into collectivistic liberalism. Like other lower-class immigrants in the large cities, they became affiliated with the Democratic party. That was quite understandable and quite reasonable. The Jews fared well under the liberalism into which they had immigrated; the potentialities of the very different collectivistic liberalism seemed to be only reasonable extensions of the liberalism from which they benefited and they saw nothing of the dangers which it held for themselves and for American society. Therein hangs the tale.

The conditions of work in the industries which they first entered and their sympathies for a progressivistic, moderately socialistic outlook drew some of them further than the then prevailing liberalism. This liberalism had many limitations but the Jews had an obligation to it as the prevalent belief of American society. American society received them and they flourished in it, certainly in comparison with the alternatives available to them in Europe. Up to the great depression of the 1930's, no harm and some good resulted from this slipping toward collectivistic liberalism for American society; the Jews lost nothing by it. American society was becoming a little more humane and its liberalism was extending its benefits to the Jews, although not without a certain amount of friction on both sides.

The Jews were also in internal conflict over the changes which they were experiencing in American society. They were renouncing the qualities and beliefs which they had developed as a "pariah people" and which had helped them to persist as a culture; they were also on their way to becoming members of a civil society which was rather different from the traditional Jewish society in which they had grown up. There was much pathos in this change. There were also two rather negative consequences: they went further in the renunciation of their own Jewish traditions than was necessary and they did not wholly assimilate the traditions of civility of the society into which they came. More specifically, many of the next generation of Jews of Eastern European parentage fell into a trough, losing much of their Jewish tradition and acquiring primarily that emergent variant of liberalism which laid stress on its distrust of authority and which at the same time expected benefits from the extension of governmental authority. They had the misfortune of coming of age in a period in which the older liberalism—the more genuinely liberal liberalism—was in discredit, and collectivistic liberalism was gaining in adherents. The liberalism of the Jews, like that of non-Jews, became a different thing from what it had been. This new kind of collectivistic liberalism, which has given liberalism a bad name and which causes traditional liberals to be misnamed as "neoconservatives," is something which the Jews should never have espoused.

I do not think that this collectivistic liberalism should be disavowed by Jews merely because a handful of blacks who claim to speak for the much larger numbers of blacks who are intended to be its beneficiaries are now acting in an extremely silly way, including in their silliness a certain amount of anti-Semitism, a spiteful sympathy with the terrorist PLO, and support for some of the worst elements in the Middle East against Israel. After all, that is what is to be expected from collectivistic liberalism, and from its reinforcement by the current of belief which led many to become fellow-travelers. This fellow-traveling outlook had attracted many Jewish intellectuals in the 1930's and 1940's and it still exists in a silent belief that Communist countries are almost always in the right and that capitalistic, more or less liberal societies are in the wrong. The Jews should renounce collectivistic liberalism and its alliances with the heirs of a dimly surviving fellow-traveling and a foolish emancipationist radicalism. They should do so not just because they should desist from offering their patronage to anti-Jewish activities and beliefs but because collectivistic liberalism and its allies are wrong and injurious to American society as well as to themselves.

The whole of American society is being severely damaged by collectivistic liberalism and the anarchic emancipationism which asserts that every impulse is sacred and that inhibition and self-restraint are tantamount to oppression. The policy of spending more than we produce, neglecting the maintenance and the renewal of our capital plant, the suspension of standards of competence and achievement in work in large organizations, the physical and moral aggravation of the public scene in the United States, and the support of iniquitous conduct by the invocation of the First Amendment are the products of collectivistic liberalism conjoined with emancipationism, which is now part of the collectivistic liberal program. Collectivistic liberalism is harmful to everyone except those who have lucrative posts in its administration and propagation; emancipationism is further disordering American society and confers benefits primarily on pornographers, vendors of drugs, and "civil-liberties" lawyers. It is not to anyone else's advantage, neither that of Jews nor that of blacks—witness the rotting away of a generation of young blacks, sustained and ruined in idleness by the self-righteously good intentions of collectivistic liberalism.

I think that Jews who are at present attached to it should cut themselves loose from this collectivistic liberalism. It is not to their interest as Jews, as Americans, or as Jewish Americans. Why should they take up a position which is ruining an imperfect but reasonably good society to which they owe so much? Why should they contribute to the ruination of American society, to the disadvantage of almost everyone in this society including in the long term blacks or Hispanics or any other ethnic minority which is being corrupted by collectivistic liberalism and deceived by the appointment of a small number of blacks or Hispanics to prominent positions?

Many Jews in the United States have contributed to the growth of collectivistic liberalism. They have added their fervor to it; they have attached to it what remains to them of secularized fragments of the prophetic tradition. But it must also be said on their behalf that they did not create it.

Richard T. Ely was not a Jew. Simon Nelson Patten was not a Jew. John Dewey was not a Jew nor was Thorstein Veblen. (I enter the name of John Dewey here with many misgivings because John Dewey was a very good man and he was not muddle-headed either; yet it cannot be denied, despite the nobility of his character and despite the excellence of his influence on his great pupils, Sidney Hook and Ernest Nagel, that John Dewey's beliefs were important ingredients of the collectivistic liberalism which is now having such disastrous consequences for our country and the world.) In the time of the New Deal, Franklin Roosevelt, Thomas Corcoran, Henry Wallace, Rexford Tugwell, Harold Ickes, Hugh Johnson, and Harry Hopkins were not Jewish. Thurman Arnold, James Landis, Walton Hamilton, and the other gravediggers of the rule of law in the United States were not Jewish either. Jews, except for Benjamin Cohen, Felix Frankfurter, Jerome Frank, and a few others, were not in the front rank of the architects and executants of the New Deal.

I am neither a believing nor an observant Jew, but I am very appreciative of my Jewish ancestry and I have a very lively sense of affinity with Jews, with *Ostjuden,* German Jews, Sephardic Jews, Ben-Israel Jews, even Cochin Jews, and I am devoted to the state of Israel partly because I have a strong feeling of kinship with its people and I regard its accomplishments in the formation of a decent society as no less admirable than those of the Swiss or the Danes or the Dutch and done under more difficult circumstances. The Jews of the Hellenistic age and of the Roman empire are very close to me. I have a visual image of my descent from these Jews of long ago.

I am pious in sentiment toward my ancestors and I am full of affection—often critical but strong—toward the generation of my parents, the poor pants-pressers, buttonhole-makers, shirtwaist-makers, cigar makers, small shopkeepers who worked so hard in a strange environment and who became patriotic Americans. I have great respect for the courage of these worthy, poor people. I have much less respect for their offspring who availed themselves of the prolific opportunities afforded by this society, discarded without regret their ancestral language, did not care to learn their history and at the same time retained the alienness of those ancestors from their society, disparaging it from the standpoint of an ideal of moral perfection which for them was embodied in the Soviet Union, one of the most disagreeable societies ever engendered by human vices. Collectivistic liberalism was made to order for this generation. Ingratitude and incivility are its attendants.

I have often thought about liberalism but not as a Jew. I think that I have never thought of American public matters from the standpoint of "how will it help the Jews?" I have never participated in any Jewish organization, and I have never felt that I should "look at things as a Jew." I am sure that my having come from an immigrant Jewish family has affected my outlook but I have always wanted to think of that outlook, such as it is, as something *sui generis,* as an outlook which must stand or fall on its own merits. I have drawn more from Aristotle and Burke and Adam Smith and Max Weber than I have from any writer who has written "from a Jewish standpoint," except perhaps for Gershom Scholem.

Nonetheless, now that COMMENTARY has asked me to reflect on whether certain recent events "warrant a reconsideration by the Jewish community in general of its traditional commitment to liberalism," I take on myself the onus of expressing the hope that my fellow Jews in the United States will turn away from collectivistic liberalism and its parasitic emancipationism and will instead reaffirm that unsystematic and inconsistent amalgam of tradition and liberalism which prevailed for a long time in the history of this country.

At present our country is in a poor way. Not all of its difficulties are attributable to collectivistic liberalism, but some of the most striking are. There is no sign of relief on the horizon. The leadership of the Democratic party is heavily burdened with the stereotypes which have been formed over the past fifty years and the deficiencies of character of those who presume to lead it do not offer a good prospect for an improvement in the near future. Will the Jews turn away from it in the next presidential election? I doubt that this will happen to any great extent; collectivistic liberalism is too engraved in their hearts for many of them to do so. And even if it were less deeply engraved, where could they turn? To the Republican party, which is also pervaded by the same ste-

reotypes, or which thinks of the illiberal glories of the 1920's, and
whose self-presenting candidates for leadership offer little assur-
ance or comfort?

I am not optimistic; but I am not without hope. Societies have
a certain toughness and resiliency because traditions are tenacious.
Our country is probably better beneath the surface of publicity
than it appears in the words and actions of our political leaders,
our publicists, and our social scientists. Maybe our educated Jews
and the rest of the educated public will begin to become aware of
this and more appreciative of that combination of tradition and
liberalism into which the Jews and other immigrants from the
1880's onward came.

THE POLITICAL DILEMMA OF AMERICAN JEWS[3]

Jews have a long history, and with that long history goes a
long memory. So it is entirely to be expected that the political loyalties and habits of mind of a Jewish community should change
very slowly—so slowly, sometimes, that an odd divergence can occur between Jewish thinking and the developing social, political,
and economic realities. It is not so much that Jews do not see what
is going on; they just do not believe it when they do see it. In politics, seeing is not always believing. Memories, and the cast of mind
into which those memories become encrusted—one can fairly call
it an ideological cast of mind—often enough will not only obscure
the reality but will actually prevail over it for a surprisingly long
time.

Something of this sort, it seems to me, is happening in the
American Jewish community today. Over the past two decades,
the political landscape with which American Jews are familiar,
and in which they are accustomed to take their bearings, has been
shifting in all sorts of unexpected ways. A sense of disorientation

[3]Reprint of an article by Irving Kristol, professor of social thought at New York University's Graduate
School of Business Administration. *Commentary.* p 23–9. Jl. '84. Reprinted from *Commentary,* 1984 by permission; all rights reserved.

has slowly been pervading the political consciousness of American Jews, causing uneasiness and discomfort. Inevitably and understandably, the initial reaction, and still the dominant reaction, is that such changes are superficial and transient, and that the old, familiar markers will enable one to make one's way. But beneath this reaction is the growing apprehension that perhaps this is not so—that perhaps the political geography of the United States has undergone a more basic realignment of its features, and that it is time for a reorientation.

Erik Erikson, in his biography of Luther, defines three critical stages in the life cycle of an individual. The first is a crisis in identity, the second a crisis of conscience (involving one's responsibility to others), and the third a crisis of integrity (a coming to terms with historical actuality). The American Jewish community is in the process of experiencing all these life-cycle crises simultaneously. No wonder there is so much bewilderment and anxiety.

Let us look at three changes in the American political landscape that were not anticipated, and that are now contributing to these crises.

The most striking change has been the emergence of Jesse Jackson as *the* political leader of American blacks. Jackson stands for black nationalism—what the media mindlessly persist in calling "black pride"—with a dash of anti-Semitism added for good measure. He is *not* a "civil-rights" leader of the familiar kind, only somewhat more militant. He has radically redefined the role of black political leadership in this country. Even if he should pass from the scene, for one reason or another, there will be no reversion to the *status quo ante*. He has, with extraordinary entrepreneurial skill, shown the way, and there will be plenty of others eager to follow.

This was not supposed to happen. American Jews had anticipated a quite different scenario to emerge from the civil-rights movement, in which they were so deeply involved. That involvement was natural because Jews, as a religious and ethnic minority, have for centuries experienced a deprivation of civil rights and are therefore keenly aware of how important it is that equality in civil rights be enjoyed by all minorities—religious, ethnic, or racial. This explains why, for most of the history of the NAACP and the Urban League, Jewish money played such a large role in keeping those institutions afloat. It also explains why so many individual Jews participated so energetically, over these past twenty years, in the civil-rights movement itself.

That movement was victorious. What are now called civil-rights issues are marginal legal quarrels, and more often than not involved women rather than blacks. So far as civil rights, traditionally understood, are concerned, there now exists a comprehensive body of law, emerging from either Congress or the courts, which defines and protects the rights of blacks. The very fact that such cities as Chicago, Philadelphia, Los Angeles, Atlanta, and Birmingham—Birmingham!—now have black mayors pretty much tells the story.

Nor is it surprising that these black mayors were elected with Jewish support, which in some cases was decisive. For until yesterday, relations between the Jewish community and the official black leadership continued to be most amiable. In Congress, black Congressmen usually voted "correctly," from the Jewish point of view, on Israel, while Jewish Congressmen usually voted "correctly" on domestic legislation that the black leadership endorsed. The black-Jewish political coalition outlasted the civil-rights movement itself, and there seemed no reason why it should not endure.

The strength of the attachment of Jews—or perhaps one should say of the major Jewish organizations and their leaders—to this coalition is best revealed by the debate over affirmative action. Affirmative action has come to be judicially and bureaucratically defined in terms of racial and ethnic quotas in hiring and firing—what has been called "positive discrimination." This is utterly repugnant, in principle, to Jews. Indeed, Jews had always felt so keenly about this sort of thing that they had fought long and hard, and in the end successfully, to prevent the introduction of religious identification in the census. To this day, all major Jewish organizations are on record as supporting "affirmative action" in the original sense of encouraging the advancement of minorities, but remain opposed to quotas. Nevertheless, once the definition of affirmative action as implying quotas became an issue of considerable importance to the black leadership, the major Jewish organizations split on whether to oppose it outright in the courts—so powerful was the desire of Jewish leaders to continue cooperating with their black counterparts.

So what went wrong. Where did Jesse Jackson come from, and why?

Well, coincident with the civil-rights movement, another social-political phenomenon occurred that was of great significance to the black community. This was the construction, by Congress, of an extensive (and expensive) range of social programs, under the rubric of the "Great Society." These programs were intended to repair the social and economic condition of American blacks, even while their political condition was being elevated to the plane of equality by the civil-rights movement. And even as the civil-rights movement succeeded, the Great Society programs failed—at least as far as most blacks were concerned. Out of this failure, Jesse Jackson emerged.

It is not to be thought that the Great Society programs were simply a waste of money. Some were, some were not. But where benefits did occur, it was largely the middle class that enjoyed them. Much of the population of the black ghettos was in no condition to exploit those benefits. It is nice to provide free lunches for poor schoolchildren, and it is unquestionably nice for the nutritionists, the food-service industry, and the farmers. But what availeth that free lunch to a black mother if her son, at the same time, gets hooked on drugs or is involved in criminal activities, while her teen-age daughter becomes pregnant? The sad truth is that the social disorganization and individual demoralization within the black ghettos have overwhelmed whatever positive effects those social programs were expected to have, or even might have had.

And there is good reason to think that the Great Society programs themselves had something to do with this social disorganization and individual demoralization. It may not be literally true that dependency (like power) tends to corrupt and that absolute dependency (like absolute power) tends to corrupt absolutely. But there is truth enough in that proposition to give pause. After all, how else explain the fact that the increasing breakdown of the black ghetto family and the proliferation of all sorts of social and individual pathologies parallel so neatly, in time and place, the institution of all those social programs? The people who devised, legislated, and applied these programs surely expected no such consequences and are now at a loss for an explanation. It is reasonable, however, to take seriously the possibility that the two phenomena have a causal connection.

In any case, it is out of the frustration of the black ghetto—frustration arising from the fact that neither the winning of political civil rights nor the enactment of those Great Society programs transformed or even ameliorated the condition of the black ghettos—that Jesse Jackson has built his mass appeal. It is worth recalling that, before becoming a candidate, he spoke with refreshing candor of the need for blacks to help themselves rather than relying on white handouts that left them mired in poverty and misery. This was not a theme that the established black leadership had the courage to enunciate. But apparently there was greater political potential in black nationalism than in black self-help, and Jackson himself has by now substituted the former for the latter.

The frustration of ghetto blacks, moreover, is as sharply felt by that portion of the black population—about half—whose condition has dramatically improved over the past decades. Racial solidarity is as natural a feeling as religious or ethnic, so it is not surprising that many middle-class blacks, especially the young and upwardly mobile, are sympathetic to Jesse Jackson. Nor is it surprising that the older, established black leadership has been so utterly disarmed before his campaign. They, after all, had bet all their chips on the civil-rights struggle and the Great Society programs. Confronted with the enduring, brutal realities of ghetto life today, they are mute and impotent.

The upshot is that the long alliance between Jewish and black organizations is coming apart. Jesse Jackson has substituted Arab money for Jewish money. In foreign policy he is pro-Third World and anti-American, pro-PLO and anti-Israel—and he is on the way to making this the quasi-official foreign policy of the black community. In domestic policy he is vaguely, but unambiguously, well to the Left of anything that one could call "liberal." And his role in future elections, which is bound to be significant, will only make things worse. He has already indicated that he will be coming to New York in 1985 to back and stump for a properly militant black candidate against Mayor Koch in the Democratic primaries. The black-Jewish polarization that would ensue is almost too scary to contemplate.

The rise of the Moral Majority is another new feature of the American landscape that baffles Jews. They did not expect it, do not understand it, and do not know what to do about it.

One of the reasons—perhaps the main reason—they do not know what to do about it is the fact that the Moral Majority is strongly pro-Israel. To say this was unexpected is a wild understatement. If one had informed American Jews fifteen years ago that there was to be a powerful revival of Protestant fundamentalism, and as a political as well as religious force, they would surely have been alarmed, since they would have assumed that any such revival might tend to be anti-Semitic and anti-Israel. But the Moral Majority is neither.

To be sure, occasionally a fundamentalist preacher will say something to the effect that God cannot be expected to heed the prayers of non-Protestant fundamentalists. At which point many Jewish organizations react in a predictable way: they sound the alarm against an incipient anti-Semitism. But the alarm rings hollow. After all, why should Jews care about the theology of a fundamentalist preacher when they do not for a moment believe that he speaks with any authority on the question of God's attentiveness to human prayer? And what do such theological abstractions matter as against the mundane fact that this same preacher is vigorously pro-Israel?

Some Jews, enmeshed in the liberal time warp, refuse to take this mundane fact seriously. They are wrong. Just how wrong they are can be seen by asking the question: how significant would it be for American Jews if the Moral Majority were *anti*-Israel? The answer is easy and inescapable: it would be of major significance. Indeed, it would generally be regarded by Jews as a very alarming matter. So it is ironic, and puzzling, that American Jews appear to be not all that interested in, and certainly not enthusiastic about, the fact that the Moral Majority is unequivocally pro-Israel.

One reason for the peculiar Jewish reaction here is that this phenomenon does not fall into the spectrum of the familiar and expected. But there are other reasons too, of considerable significance in their own way. For the Moral Majority is simultaneously committed to a set of "social issues"—school prayer, anti-abortion, the relation of church and state in general—that tend to evoke a hostile reaction among most (though not all) American Jews. How does one go about balancing the pros and cons of this matter? And to what degree is this hostile reaction itself worthy of some second thoughts?

That balancing should not, in truth, require much intellectual effort. From a purely expediential point of view, it is obvious that the campaign of the Moral Majority around these "social issues" is meeting with practically no success, and so there is little reason for Jewish alarm. Neither Congress nor (more important) the judiciary is at all forthcoming, and the Reagan administration has got absolutely nowhere in its espousal of these issues. In contrast, anti-Israel sentiment has been distinctly on the rise, and the support of the Moral Majority could, in the near future, turn out to be decisive for the very existence of the Jewish state. This is the way the Israeli government has struck its own balance vis-à-vis the Moral Majority, and it is hard to see why American Jews should come up with a different bottom line.

But the expediential point of view is not enough if the Moral Majority's support of Israel is not to wither and die on the vine. That will happen if it continues to evoke so muffled and embarrassed a response from the American Jewish community. American Jews really do need to revise their thinking about some, at least, of these controversial social issues, even from the point of view of expediency. Moreover, it is becoming ever more clear that it is time they did so in any case, Moral Majority or no Moral Majority.

Ever since the Holocaust and the emergence of the state of Israel, American Jews have been reaching toward a more explicit and meaningful Jewish identity and have been moving away from the universalist secular humanism that was so prominent a feature of their prewar thinking. But while American Jews want to become more Jewish, they do not want American Christians to become more Christian. This is an untenable point of view.

First, because of the hypocrisy involved. Why should there be a Hanukkah candelabrum at Central Park, as there is, but no Christmas crèche? Second, because the quest for a religious identity is not confined to Jews. It is, in the postwar world, a general phenomenon experienced by Jews, Christians, and Muslims alike. It does not seem, moreover, to be a passing phenomenon but rather derives from an authentic crisis—a moral and spiritual crisis as well as a crisis in Western liberal-secular thought. Is there any point in Jews hanging on, dogmatically and hypocritically, to their opinions of yesteryear when it is a new era we are confronting? Is it not time for Jews to sit back, curb their habitual reflexes about the "proper" relations of state and religion in the United States, and think seriously about how they can most comfortably exist (and survive) in a world in which religious identity will become increasingly important? In short, is it not time for an agonizing reappraisal?

The relation of American Jews to American foreign policy is, every day, becoming more and more bizarre, more and more tormented by self-contradiction. It is a situation that cannot last. Sooner or later, American Jews are going to have to make very hard choices—hard, because they will go against a deeply imprinted grain.

To select one issue that is profoundly symptomatic because it touches on such a sensitive ideological nerve: the United Nations and the attitude of our major Jewish organizations to it.

We all know—one would have to be deaf and dumb not to know—that the UN is, above all, an organization bent on delegitimizing, even eventually destroying, the state of Israel. More than half the time, the UN and its associated organizations are busy pursuing this mission. The rest of the time they are preoccupied with serving as a forum for a Third World critique of the United States, and of the West in general, of which Israel is perceived (correctly) to be an integral part. "Zionism is racism" is a doctrine officially proclaimed by the UN, while at no time has the UN shown the slightest interest in protecting the rights of Jews (and other minorities) in the Soviet Union or in Muslim nations.

It would seem to follow logically that the American Jewish community should be hostile to the UN, should like to see the

United States dissociate itself from it to the greatest possible degree, should even wish to see it vanish from our political horizon. Why not, after all? But logic, apparently, plays very little role in defining Jewish attitudes toward the United Nations. Nostalgia for what it was once hoped the UN would be is stronger than the clear perception of what the UN indubitably is. If ever there was a case of a group of people desperately evading the most obvious of political realities, this is it.

To be sure, Jews (like most other Americans) are full of admiration for Daniel Patrick Moynihan or Jeane Kirkpatrick when they boldly stand up for Israel—and America—at the UN. They are honored with plaques, scrolls, honorary degrees, banquets, etc. But that is as far as it goes. Just let anyone suggest that the Jewish reaction to the UN, as it now exists, should go somewhat farther and, suddenly, all the Jewish organizations have lost their tongue.

When efforts are made in Congress to cut the American financial contribution to the UN—we now provide 25 percent of the budget—the American Jewish community remains on the sidelines. When the Reagan administration decided to withdraw from that scandalous entity called UNESCO, the American Jewish community could think of nothing supportive to say, at least openly. Even Ambassador Charles Lichenstein's semi-jocular remark to the effect that, if the UN wished to relocate its headquarters elsewhere, he would be on the dock waving an enthusiastic farewell, was greeted by the Jewish community with a frigid silence. Meanwhile, the United Nations Association, along with other organizations that "educate" people toward a "positive" view of the UN, are financed most generously by Jewish contributors.

Here the discrepancy between the reality and Jewish ideological obstinacy is positively stunning. The UN has become a very different organization from what Jews and Jewish organizations, in the immediate postwar years, anticipated and hoped it would be. They certainly never expected that the covenant against "genocide," for which American Jewry lobbied in the UN so persistently and, finally, successfully, would serve as a basis for attacks against Israel, as it is, repeatedly. The actuality has diverged wildly from the dream. But the dream still exercises its dominion over the Jewish imagination.

The vision of a "community of nations" living peaceably under international law, so eloquently articulated by Immanuel Kant in the 18th century, has been an organic part of the ideology of Western liberalism ever since. It has had a special appeal to Jews, both because of its biblical roots and because Jews, as Jews, would obviously be much more secure and comfortable in such a world. No single ethnic or religious group in the United States has produced such a disproportionate number of scholars in the field of international law as have Jews, and no other group has been so reluctant to recognize that this messianic vision, when applied to political actualities, has proved to be political utopianism, wishful thinking.

It is not that international law itself is in essence utopian. The emergence, in the two centuries *preceding* Kant, of principles of decent international behavior was a genuine contribution toward making international relations less anarchic, less "Machiavellian," less casually brutal than they had been or otherwise would have been. But this *pre*-Kantian conception of international law was much more modest in its ambitions and more realistic in its assumptions than the notion of international law we are familiar with. It recognized, for instance, that the intervention of nations in the affairs of other nations was both proper and inevitable under certain conditions, and that the violation of national frontiers could not always be classified as immoral "aggression." To the degree that international law has any substantial meaning in the world today, it rests on this pre-Kantian basis rather than on the kind of grandiose principles associated with the League of Nations and the United Nations.*

An extraordinary number of Jews, however, remain loyal to those grandiose principles. As a result, their thinking about foreign affairs is incoherent to an equally extraordinary degree.

---

*This older, but still modern, conception of international law is very clearly laid out in Sir Thomas More's *Utopia* (1515). Its most thoughtful application is to be found in John Stuart Mill's essay, "A Few Words on Non-Intervention" (1859). The occasion was Russian intervention in Hungary (!) and the problem was the appropriate British response. It is an essay whose conclusions are quite consistent with the Reagan administration's policies in Central America.

When Israel bombed and destroyed the Iraqi nuclear reactor most American Jews realized that this was a sensible thing to do and that there was nothing "illegal" or "immoral" about the act—but they could not figure out a way to say this. Approval at the personal level was matched by embarrassed double-talk at the official level as Jewish leaders tried to talk their way out of a rhetorical trap of their own construction.

In addition to incoherence, there is positive schizophrenia. All Jews would be pleased if Ronald Reagan were publicly to reproach the Soviet Union on the issue of Jewish emigration, but would be less happy if his reproach were aimed at the suppression of all religious freedoms under that "godless" regime. This, it is felt, might be construed as undue intervention in Soviet Russia's internal affairs, and might "worsen international tensions," "aggravate the cold war," etc., etc.

One can muddle through with such incoherence and schizophrenia for a while, but sooner or later the world demands that one talk sense. Such a demand is being imposed on American Jews today. The older liberal internationalism, which was the basis of American foreign policy after the end of World War II and the basis of our membership in the United Nations, is rapidly disintegrating. The Third World uses the UN when it can, ignores it when convenient. So do the Soviet Union and the other Communist countries. There is no "community of nations," and the grand principles of the UN Charter are cynically abused for the purposes of *Realpolitik*. The United States is being forced to choose between being an active, great power in the world as it exists, or gradually retiring into a quasi-isolationism that leaves our moral purity undefiled and the world to its own devices.

The Democratic party today, and especially its most liberal wing, is clearly moving toward this second alternative. It is a movement made all the easier by the unspoken (because uneasy) liberal assumption that left-wing totalitarian movements, paying lip-service to principles that have a superficial affinity with liberal ideas, will evolve into less totalitarian and more liberal regimes. This assumption flies in the face of the fact that the most evident political reality of the 20th century is the revolt *against* the liberal economic and political order and the liberal ideal of self-government. That this revolt is sometimes explicitly "reactionary" or sometimes "progressive" in its political metaphysics is of interest to historians of ideas, but has little bearing on the construction of foreign policy. Indeed, what is most striking in recent decades is the *convergence* between yesteryear's totalitarian governments of the Right and today's totalitarian regimes of the Left. The similarities between Castro's Cuba and Mussolini's Italy are far more striking than their differences.

Isolationism has a strong traditional appeal to the American people and one can understand why it should reemerge today, or why the prospect of fighting "dirty little wars" in remote places should be so repugnant. What is difficult to understand is why American Jews seem to be among those who are not shocked and appalled by this new trend. Can anyone believe that an American government which, in righteous moralistic *hauteur,* refuses to intervene to prevent a Communist takeover of Central America, will intervene to counterbalance Soviet participation in an assault on Israel? Can anyone believe that the American people could make sense of such contradictory behavior? Yet a large number of American Jews, perhaps even a majority, appear to believe it.

Have these Jews taken leave of their reason? Of course not. It is simply that their thinking is beclouded by anachronistic presuppositions about the kind of world we live in and about the appropriate responses by the United States to the kind of world we live in. This *real* world is rife with conflict and savagery. It is a world in which liberalism is very much on the defensive, in which public opinion runs in the grooves established by power, in which people back winners not losers, and in which winners not losers provide the models of the future. In such a world, we are constrained to take our allies where and how we find them—even if they are authoritarian (e.g., Turkey), even if they are totalitarian (e.g., China).

If American Jews truly wish to be noninterventionist, they have to cease being so concerned with Israel, with Jews in the Soviet Union, or indeed with Jews anywhere else. To demand that an American government be interventionist exclusively on behalf of Jewish interests and none other—well, to state that demand is to reveal its absurdity. Yet most of our major Jewish organizations have ended up maneuvering themselves into exactly this position. They cannot even bring themselves openly to support the indispensable precondition for the exercise of American influence on behalf of Jewish interests in the world: a large and powerful military establishment that can, if necessary, fight and win dirty, little (or not so little) wars in faraway places. It is the winning or losing of such wars that will determine the kind of world our children inherit—not striking pious postures or exuding moralistic rhetoric.

To quote Erik Erikson once again:

In some period of his history, and in some phases of his life cycle, man needs a new ideological orientation as surely and as sorely as he must have light and air.

Today is such a period for the American Jewish community. For two centuries, Western Jewry has been wedded to the intellectual traditions and political movements that had their roots in the Enlightenment. This was understandable and inevitable, since it was this current of thought and these movements—liberal or Left-of-liberal—which achieved religious toleration and civic equality for Jews. Conservative thinkers and conservative political parties tended to be hostile to Jewish aspirations, or at best coolly indifferent. In the United States, founded as it was in the flush of Enlightenment enthusiasm, the division between liberalism and conservatism was never that pregnant with meaning for Jews. Nevertheless, as relatively new immigrants, Jews found liberal opinion and liberal politicians more congenial in their attitudes, more sensitive to Jewish concerns. For the most part they still do. The kind of social discrimination—in country clubs, business luncheon clubs, within the corporate community generally—that Jews experience even today is generally at the hands of people who express conservative opinions and are likely to vote Republican. This form of discrimination affects only a fraction of the Jewish population—but that fraction includes those upper-middle-class, affluent Jews who are active in community affairs and provide the leadership of Jewish organizations.

Still, the world changes and will continue to change no matter how stubbornly Jews stick their heads in the sand and hope that yesteryear's realities will return. The American Jewish community needs the light of reason and the refreshing air of candid discourse if the world is not to pass it by. It must begin to see things as they are, not as it would like them to be.

One of the things it must see, on the domestic level, is that the liberal consensus and the liberal coalition that have dominated American politics since the inauguration of Franklin D. Roosevelt are disintegrating—at least so far as Jews are concerned. The blacks may or may not remain members of this coalition—one presumes they probably will—but if they do, it will be on a new set of terms. Though a great many Jews will gallantly try to swallow these terms, in the end the American Jewish community will gag on them. Can anyone doubt that, henceforth, the black caucus in Congress will be inclined to think that military or economic aid for Israel can be better spent for social programs in the ghettos? This is what Jesse Jackson thinks, this is what he says, and what Jesse Jackson thinks and says today is what the black caucus will think and say tomorrow. And can anyone doubt that, under a Mondale or Hart Presidency, our next ambassador to the UN will be more like Andrew Young than Jeane Kirkpatrick? All of these terms have been set by Jesse Jackson, and he means them most seriously. He must mean them seriously if he is to maintain his political leadership of the black community. His mission has been to incorporate a Third World view of politics into the American political spectrum, especially into the portion of that spectrum dealing with foreign affairs, and if he cannot do this within the Democratic party he will either desert that party or his enthusiastic followers will desert him. His die is cast.

But the increasing and tragic polarization between blacks and Jews is only one feature of the disengagement of the liberal coalition from Jewish interests. Another is the changes that are occurring in one of the traditional bastions of that coalition, namely, the trade unions. This reality is masked by the fact that the current head of the AFL-CIO, Lane Kirkland, is an old-fashioned liberal, a Henry Jackson type of liberal—in short, the kind of liberal Jews have cooperated with so amiably in the past. But Kirkland, alas, is not forever, and one can already see the ground shifting beneath his feet. It is, so far as American Jews are concerned, an ominous shift.

To begin with, there is the little noticed fact that the so-called "Jewish unions" are on the verge of disappearing. The Amalgamated Clothing Workers, the International Ladies Garment Workers, the American Federation of Teachers still have Jewish leaders with close ties to the Jewish community. But their membership is already overwhelmingly black, Hispanic, and Oriental, and future leaders will have no reason to be especially concerned with Jewish issues.

Meanwhile, organized labor itself is moving away from the nonpolitical tradition of Samuel Gompers and is developing closer official ties with the Democratic party. As this happens, the unions themselves naturally take on the ideological coloration of their political allies. If one wants to get a sense of what this can mean, one has simply to look at the "educational materials" prepared by the National Education Association—once a professional association, now more a union—and observe how "fair" it is to the PLO, how coolly skeptical it is of Israel's virtues. The AFL-CIO's executive council, too, is moving to distance itself from Lane Kirkland's "old-fashioned" views on foreign policy. All in all, organized labor in the United States is reshaping itself in the mold of European trade-unionism, with an organic connection to a social-democratic party and with an ideology to suit. That ideology—as expressed, for instance, in the conferences and publications of the Socialist International—is pro-Third World, anti-Israel. It is now far more Left than it is traditionally liberal. But then, liberalism itself, in the United States as elsewhere, has moved distinctly to the Left in the past two decades.

This shift is very evident in a third pillar of the older liberal coalition, that class of people we call "the intellectuals"—those in academia, the media, and the foundation world. These men and women used to be predominantly liberal. Today, it is fair to describe most of them as being to the Left of the older liberalism. In the case of the media, the transition has been obvious enough, as reportage on Middle Eastern events has made clear. Here, too, we are witnessing a process that is not peculiarly American. In Britain, France, Germany, Italy, the media are even more highly critical of Israel, compassionate toward the PLO. We are witnessing the coming of age, the accession to positions of power and influence in all the institutions of the media, of the youthful rebels of the 1960's. Their attitudes may have softened somewhat, but they have not been significantly reshaped.

In the case of academia, these attitudes have actually sharpened rather than softened. The academic community today, populated by the graduate students of the 1960's, and insulated from worldly experience, is more openly and vigorously left-wing than ever before in American history. The most influential intellectual tendency among academicians today is Marxism, in a dozen or more different versions, some of them so far from the original as to perplex older Marxists, but all of them pointing in the same political direction. Just what that direction is may be inferred from the fact—and it is a fact—that an invitation to Ambassador Jeane Kirkpatrick to speak on campus will cause intense controversy in faculty councils, with quite a few professors going so far as to encourage student harassment should she appear. Meanwhile, such invitations go out routinely to Third World spokesmen, whose anti-Israel and anti-American remarks are listened to respectfully.

In short, while American Jews have for the most part persisted in their loyalty to the politics of American liberalism, that politics has blandly and remorselessly distanced itself from them. For the first time in living memory, Jews are finding themselves in the old condition of being politically homeless. It is possible, though far from certain, that Jews in the West will find a new home, however uncomfortable, in the conservative and neoconservative politics that, in reaction to liberalism's leftward drift, seems to be gaining momentum. But whether this conservatism will be keenly enough interested in Jews to offer tolerable lodging to them is itself an open question.

What is no longer an open question is the dissociation that has occurred, and is daily occurring, between the American Jewish community and its traditional allies. That is an established fact—and one that American Jews must candidly confront.

BIBLIOGRAPHY

An asterisk (*) preceding a reference indicates that the article or part of it has been reprinted in this book.

BOOKS AND PAMPHLETS

American Jewish Archives. Jews, Judaism and the American constitution. '82.

Ashabranner, Brent. The new Americans. Dodd, Mead. '83.

Ashmore, Harry S. Hearts and minds: the anatomy of racism from Roosevelt to Reagan. McGraw-Hill. '82.

Beardslee, William R. The way out must lead in: life histories in the civil rights movement. Lawrence Hill. '83.

Benedict, Ruth. Race. Greenwood Press. '82.

Berlin, William S. On the edge of politics. Greenwood Press. '78.

Blalock, Hubert M. Race and ethnic relations. Prentice Hall. '82.

Bouvier, Leon F. and Davis, Cary B. The future racial composition of the United States. Demographic Information Services Center of the Population Reference Bureau, Washington, D.C. '82.

Bragdon, Henry Wilkinson and Pittemger, John C. The pursuit of justice. Crowell-Collier Press. '69.

Bullock, Charles S. and Rodgers, Harrell R., eds. Black political attitudes. Markham. '72.

Bullock, Charles S. and Rodgers, Harrell R. Racial equality in America. Goodyear. '75.

Cartwright, Joseph H. The triumph of Jim Crow. University of Tennessee Press. '76.

Cashmore, Ernest and Troyna, Barry. Introduction to race relations. Routledge and Kegan. '83.

Cassity, Michael J. Chains of fear: American race relations since reconstruction. Greenwood Press. '83.

Casstevens, Thomas W. Politics, housing, and race relations. Institute of Governmental Studies, University of California. '67.

Cavanagh, Thomas E. Race and political strategy. Joint Center for Political Studies. '83.

Clausen, Edwin and Bermingham, Jack. Pluralism, racism, and public policy: the search for equality. G. K. Hall. '81.

Comas, Juan. Racial myths. Greenwood Press. '76.

Corringham, Clement, ed. Race, poverty, and the urban underclass. Lexington Books. '82.

Corwin, A. F. Immigration and immigrants: perspectives on Mexican labor immigration to the U.S. Greenwood Press. '78.

Crewe, Ivor. The politics of race. Wiley. '75.

Curtis, Lynn A. Violence, race, and culture. Heath. '77.

Daniels, Roger. The politics of prejudice. University of California Press. '77.

Detweiler, Robert and Kornweibel, Theodore. Slave and citizen: a critical annotated bibliography on slavery and race relations in the Americas. Campanile. '83.

Du Bois, W. E. B. Dusk of dawn: an essay toward an autobiography of a race concept. Kraus International. '75.

Eisinger, Peter K. Patterns of interracial politics. Academic Press. '76.

El Azhary, M. S. Political cohesion of American Jews in American politics. University Press of America. '80.

Elazar, Daniel Judah and Cohen, Stuart. The Jewish polity. Indiana University Press. '84.

Feagin, Joe R. Racial and ethnic relations. Prentice Hall. '84.

Field, Phyllis F. The politics of race in New York. Cornell University Press. '82.

Foner, Philip Sheldon. American socialism and black Americans. Greenwood Press. '77.

Foner, Philip S., ed. Paul Robeson speaks: writing, speeches, interviews 1918-1974. Brunner-Mazel. '78.

Fuchs, Lawrence H. The political behavior of American Jews. Greenwood Press. '80.

Garver, Susan. Coming to North America: from Mexico, Cuba, and Puerto Rico. Delacorte Press. '81.

Goodman, Walter and Goodman, Elaine. The rights of the people: the major decisions of the Warren court. Farrar, Straus & Giroux. '71.

Goodwin, Carole. The Oak Park strategy: community control of racial change. University of Chicago Press. '79.

Grose, Peter L. Israel in the mind of America. Schocken Books. '84.

Haskins, James. The new Americans. Enslow Publishers. '82.

Haws, Robert, ed. The age of segregation: race relations in the South, 1890-1945. University Press of Mississippi. '78.

Holden, Mathew. The divisible republic. Abelard-Shuman. '73.

Karnig, Albert and Welch, Susan. Black representation and urban policy. University of Chicago Press. '81.

King, Martin Luther. Why we can't wait. Harper and Row. '64.

Kirp, David. Just schools: the idea of racial equality in American education. University of California Press. '82.

Leggett, John. Race, class, and political consciousness. Schenkman. '72.

Lewis, Anthony. Portrait of a decade: the second American revolution. Random House. '64.

Liebman, Arthur. Jews and the left. Wiley. '79.

Marable, Manning. Race, reform and rebellion. University Press of Mississippi. '84.

McAdam, Doug. Political process and the development of black insurgency 1930–1970. University of Chicago Press. '82.

Miles, Robert. Racism and migrant labour: a critical text. Routledge and Kegan. '83.

Mindel, Charles H. and Habenstein, Robert. Ethnic families in America. Elsevier. '76.

Mintz, Frank P. The liberty lobby and the American right. Greenwood Press. '85.

Montagu, Ashley. Man's most dangerous myth: the fallacy of race. Oxford University Press. '74.

Ogbu, J. U. Minority education and caste: the American system in cross-cultural perspective. Academic Press. '78.

Peirce, Neal R. The deep south states of America. Norton. '74.

Polenberg, Richard. One nation divisible: class, race, and ethnicity in the United States since 1938. Viking. '81.

Portes, Alejandro and Bach, Robert L. Latin journey. University of California Press. '84.

President's National Advisory Commission on Civil Disorders. '68. Comparing the immigrant and Negro experience.

Preston, Michael B. and Henderson, Lenneal J., eds. The new black politics: the search for political power. Longman. '82.

Reich, Michael. Racial inequality: a political-economic analysis. Princeton University Press. '81.

Robinson, Cedric J. Black Marxism: the making of the black radical tradition. Biblio Dist. '83.

Rubinstein, W. D. The left, the right and the Jews. Universe Books. '82.

Ruchames, Louis. Race, jobs and politics. Negro Universities Press. '71.

Rustin, Bayard. Down the line. Quadrangle. '71.

Solomon, Gus J. The Jewish role in the American civil rights movements. World Jewish Congress. '67.

Sorin, Gerald. The prophetic minority. Indiana University Press. '84.

Sowell, Thomas. The economics and politics of race: an international perspective. Morrow. '83.

Suttles, Gerald D. The social construction of communities. University of Chicago Press. '72.

U.S. Commission on Civil Rights. '76. Puerto Ricans in the continental United States: an uncertain future.

Washington, Joseph R. Jews in black perspectives. Fairleigh Dickinson University Press, Associated University Presses. '84.

Weyl, Nathaniel. The Jew in American politics. Arlington House. '68.

Willette, JoAnne and others. The demographic and socioeconomic characteristics of the Hispanic population in the United States: 1950-1980. U.S. Department of Health and Human Services. '82.

Woodward, C. Vann. American counterpoint: slavery and racism in the North-South dialogue. Oxford University Press. '83.

Young, Richard P., ed. Roots of rebellion. Harper & Row. '70.

Zinn, Howard. SNCC, the new abolitionists. Beacon. '64.

PERIODICALS

American Behavioral Scientist. 757-72. Jl./Ag. '83. Race and ethnic relations: the elite policy response in capitalist societies. James Fendrich.

American Sociological Review. 518-32. Ag. '82. Whites' beliefs about blacks' opportunity. James Klugel and Eliot R. Smith.

Atlantic. 253:62+. F. '84. Ronald Reagan and the techniques of deception. James Nathan Miller.

Black Enterprise. 13:13. Ja. '83. 1982 election returns. Emile Milne.

Black Enterprise. 13:11. F. '83. Blacks exhibit clout at the ballot box. Earl G. Graves.

Black Enterprise. 13:40-2+. Mr. '83. Beyond the ballot box. Bebe Moore Campbell.

Black Enterprise. 13:17. My. '83. Black power at the polls. Frank McRae.

Black Enterprise. 14:20. N. '83. Black GOP warns Reagan. Derek T. Dingle.

Black Enterprise. 14:36-9+. Mr. '84. The power of the black vote: election 1984. Derek T. Dingle and David C. Ruffin.

Black Scholar. p 2–15. Fall '82. Reaganism, racism, and reaction: black political realignment in the 1980s. Manning Marable.

Business Week. p 32. Jl. 4, '83. Hispanic power arrives at the ballot box.

Center Magazine. 16:8–26. My./Je. '83. American Jews and the state of Israel. Harry Molotch.

Christian Century. 100:238. Mr. 16, '83. Is race an issue in the Chicago election? James M. Wall.

Christian Century. 100:1110+. N. 30, '83. The dialectics of affirmative action. Wanda Warren Berry.

Christianity Today. 27:34–7. My. 20, '83. Why black brethren embrace politics. Randy Frame.

Civil Rights Research Review. p 15–26. Spring/Summer '81. Analyzing trends in sexual and racial inequality in employment. Hugh Lautard.

*Commentary. p 15+. Ja. '80. Liberalism & the Jews: a symposium.

*Commentary. 78:23–9. Jl. '84. The political dilemma of American Jews. Irving Kristol.

Daedalus. Spring '81. American Indians, blacks, Chicanos, and Puerto Ricans.

Daedalus. Spring '81. Chicanos in the United States: a history of exploitation and resistance. Leobardo Estrada and others.

Ebony. 39:108–10. N. '83. The black vote: the new power in politics. Harold Washington.

*Esquire. 99:47+. My. '83. The Latinization of America. Thomas B. Morgan.

Essence. 14:56. Jl. '83. A coalition with clout. Barbara A. Reynolds.

Essence. 14:38. N. '83. Our clout at the ballot box. Cheryl Everette.

Essence. 15:36+. My. '84. Blacks hold key to election win.

Harper's. 267:30+. D. '83. Revolt on the Veldt. Carole A. Douglis and Stephen M. Davis.

Howard Law Journal. no. 3. p 381–428. '80. Assault on affirmative action: the delusion of a color blind America. Herbert O. Reid.

Intercom. N./D. '81. The U.S.-Hispanic population: a question of definition. Carl Haub.

Journal of Negro Education. p 90–100. Spring '82. Urban public school desegregation: the reproduction of normative white domination. John H. Stanfield.

Journal of Politics. p 2–23. F. '81. Presidential leverage over social movements: the Johnson White House and civil rights. Bruce Miroff.

Journal of Public and International Affairs. p 115–50. Spring '83. Minorities in the eighties.

Journal of Public and International Affairs. p 176–89. Spring '83. The Reagan administration and the resurgence of racism (interview with Roger Wilkins).

Macleans. 96:20–1. Ap. 25, '83. The message of Chicago. Val Ross.

Macleans. 96:16–17. Jl. 25, '83. Reagan and the black vote. Michael Posner.

Macleans. 96:21. Ag. 22, '83. Reagan hunts for the Hispanic vote. William Lowther.

Macleans. 97:37+. Ap. 30, '84. Restoring blacks' faith in politics. Michael Posner.

Macleans. 97:32–3. My. 14, '84. A surge of Hispanic power. Michael Posner.

*Miami Herald. p 6A. Ja. 8, '84. Hispanic vote: sleeping giant awakening. Barbara Gutierrez.

Nation. 236:205+. F. 19, '83. The return of the big bambino. Lenora E. Berson and David Moberg.

Nation. 236:362+. Mr. 26, '83. Causes without lawyers—why attorneys won't take civil rights cases. Lewis M. Steel.

Nation. 236:466. Ap. 16, '83. The mayor's race.

*Nation. 237:521+. N. 26, '83. Black power in the age of Jackson. Andrew Kopkind.

*National Journal. p 2410–16. N. 19, '83. The Hispanic vote—parties can't gamble that the sleeping giant won't awaken. Dick Kirschten.

*National Review. 30:92–4. Ja. 20, '78. Ethnic politics. William Peterson.

*National Review. 32:1250+. O. 17, '80. How should American Jews vote? Jacob Neusner.

National Review. 35:476. Ap. 29, '83. Chicago '82, America '84.

National Review. 35:537–8. My. 13, '83. Black electoral power.

Negro History Bulletin. 46:60–2. Ap./My./Je. '83. The election of an Ohio congressman. Philip A. Grant, Jr.

*Negro History Bulletin. 46:72–3+. Jl./Ag./S. '83. What's next? Julian Bond.

New Republic. 188:12–13. Ap. 18, '83. Racial brush fires.

New Republic. 188:4. Ap. 25, '83. White Chicago.

New Republic. 188:11+. My. 2, '83. Chicago squeaker. Stephen Chapman.

New Republic. 190:10+. Ja. 30, '84. Celebrating Dr. King's birthday. Robert Weisbrot.

New Republic. 190:11–13. Ap. 30, '84. Jackson and the pols. Barbara Reynolds.

New York. 16:38–45. O. 10, '83. The power next time. Joe Klein.

New York. 16:36+. O. 24, '83. Jesse Jackson's new math. Michael Kramer.

*New York Times. p E5. Ap. 1, '84. Ethnic divisions surface in the campaign. John Herbers.

*New York Times Magazine. p 34–9. N. 27, '83. Voting: the new black power. Paul Delaney.

New York Times Magazine. p 22–8+. F. 5, '84. New powers, new politics. Theodore H. White.

New Yorker. 59:118+. Ap. 11, '83. Been down so long it looks like up. Andy Logan.

New Yorker. 59:88+. My. 9, '83. Setbacks. Andy Logan.

New Yorker. 60:34+. Ag. 13, '84. A political journal. Elizabeth Drew.

*Newsweek. 87:53. Ap. 26, '76. The politics of ethnicity. Kenneth L. Woodward.

Newsweek. 101:23–4+. Ap. 11, '83. The new black politics. David M. Alpern.

Newsweek. 102:23–4. Jl. 4, '83. Hispanic power at the polls. Jonathan Alter.

Newsweek. 102:14–15. Jl. 25, '83. Courting the black vote. Mark Starr.

Newsweek. 102:50+. N. 14, '83. What makes Jesse Jackson run?

Newsweek. 103:38. Ap. 16, '84. Black and white in California. Mark L. Stebbins.

Newsweek. 103:23. Ap. 30, '84. Now, the Jackson reaction.

Newsweek. 103:12–13. Je. 18, '84. The plight of the Jewish voter. Arthur Hertzberg.

Social Service Review. p 511–34. D. '78. Patterns of welfare use. Martin Rein and Lee Rainwater.

Society. 21:80+. N./D. '83. Inner-city dislocations. William Julius Wilson.

Society. 21:35–40. N./D. '83. Racial and class boundaries. Elijah Anderson.

Society. 21:48–53. N./D. '83. Slicing the political pie. Ira Katznelson.

Time. p 112. O. 16, '78. Hispanic Americans: soon the biggest minority.

Time. 121:24–5. Je. 6, '83. From protest to politics. Maureen Dowd.

Time. 122:20–4+. Ag. 22, '83. Seeking votes and clout. Walter Isaacson.

Time. 123:84. Ap. 16, '84. The powers of racial example. Lance Morrow.

U.S. News & World Report. 89:71-2. O. 6, '80. Black churches try for political comeback. James Mann.

U.S. News & World Report. 93:40-2. S. 27, '82. Minorities' drive thrown into reverse? David A. Wiessler.

U.S. News & World Report. 94:59. F. 21, '83. Chicago's bare-knuckle race for mayor. John W. Mashek.

U.S. News & World Report. 94:20-1. F. 28, '83. For many U.S. Jews: Israel yes, Begin no.

U.S. News & World Report. 94:15. Mr. 7, '83. Chicago's black voters send a signal.

U.S. News & World Report. 94:16. Ap. 11, '83. Racial politics flares in Chicago.

U.S. News & World Report. 94:69-70. Ap. 18, '83. Blacks' new bid for bigger role in politics. John W. Mashek.

U.S. News & World Report. 94:23-4. Je. 13, '83. Cubans to Reagan: we won't back down. Carl J. Migdail.

U.S. News & World Report. 95:48-9. Ag. 22, '83. Hispanics set their sights on ballot box. John W. Mashek and Sarah Peterson.

U.S. News & World Report. 95:15. S. 26, '83. Why politicians cry "Viva Hispanics."

U.S. News & World Report. 95:35+. D. 19, '83. Jesse Jackson shakes up race for White House. Jeannye Thornton with John Mashek.

Village Voice. p 50+. F. 14, '84. The reds and the blacks (book review). Paul Berman.

Vital Issues. 31:50+. Enterprise zones. Mark G. Michaelsen.

Vital Speeches. p 162+. Ja. 1, '84. The have not constituencies. Kevin C. Gottlieb.

Wall Street Journal. Je. 9, '82. Latins rise in numbers in U.S. but don't win influence or affluence. Marilyn Chase.

*Washington Post. Mr. 25, '84. Hispanics' political star ascending. Haynes Johnson and Thomas B. Edsall.

*Washington Post. Ag. 14, '84. The battle for Ellis Island. Michael Barone.

World Press Review. 30:43. N. '83. Wooing the Hispanics. Carlos Agudelo.